Praise for

CHANGE YOUR GAME

"The most engaging personal development book you will ever pick up."

Ryan Gottfredson, leadership professor and *Wall Street Journal* best-selling author of *The Elevated Leader*

"In a world that constantly demands new ideas and fresh perspectives, this book is an essential guide for the next generation of leaders. With engaging insights and practical wisdom, it not only inspires young people to step into leadership roles but also equips them with the tools to lead with authenticity, resilience, and empathy. This is more than just a book—it's a call to action for today's youth to rise above challenges, embrace their unique strengths, and make a positive impact on the world. A must-read for anyone who is ready to lead with purpose!"

Kirby Amacker, Boys & Girls Clubs of America National Area Council Committee; board member, Boys & Girls Clubs of Benton and Franklin Counties

"At a time when we are desperate for passionate and principled leadership from passionate and principled leaders, Chad Mitchell has produced a wonderfully direct, effective, and practical approach to leadership. And do not let the title fool you—Chad's approach to leadership development is something both young and mature leaders can benefit from. So read it, ponder it, and then go out and do it!"

John P. LaFemina, PhD, retired executive, Battelle Memorial Institute; board member, Boys & Girls Clubs of Benton and Franklin Counties and Boys & Girls Clubs Area Council for Washington and Alaska

"Having worked closely with Chad on our law firm's executive leadership team (and having been law partners for seventeen years), I've witnessed firsthand his ability to mentor and lead with heart, humility, humor, and an unfailing commitment to excellence. This book is a powerful reflection of those values—an inspiring guide that empowers young people to step into leadership with confidence and purpose. With his conversational and engaging style, Chad speaks directly to youth in a way that is both relatable and motivating. I got chills reading Chad's book. I wish he had written it sooner so my kids could have benefited from it during those crucial years."

Kristin Anger, CEO, Summit Law Group, PLLC

"This is more than a book—it's a trusted guide for the next generation of young leaders. *Change Your Game* shows young people how to take control of their lives and makes the concept of leadership feel personal, possible, and worthy of their time. Chad Mitchell understands youth in a way few adults do, and he speaks their language with clarity and compassion.

I wish every young person would read *Change Your Game*. It's wise without being preachy, practical without being boring, and very, very honest. If you've ever wondered how you can help build a better future for your children, give them this book. It will show them how *they* can lead the way."

Scott Remy, father of three; former head of communications, Nestlé USA and DineEquity (Applebee's/IHOP)

"*Change Your Game* captures powerful, universal principles and delivers them through a simple but profound shift in perspective: Life isn't something that happens to you—it's a game you choose to play. This book gives young people the mindset and tools to transform themselves with clarity, courage, and purpose—and in turn, transform the lives of others and the world around them. It's total empowerment and exactly what the rising generation needs right now."

Elijah Stanfield, cocreator and illustrator of *The Tuttle Twins*

"Chad Mitchell could teach a lamppost how to be a dynamic leader. I've watched him activate and engage youth as a coach and mentor for years. This book is a culminating masterpiece of decades of Chad's passion and commitment to our nation's youth.

Chad's elevation of empathetic listening is perhaps the book's most important takeaway. This concept alone could revolutionize a generation of young leaders by teaching them how to listen and speak with uniting and empowering affirmation and acceptance.

By offering a refreshing perspective on mistakes, reframing them not as failures but as integral parts of the journey of growth, *Change Your Game* teaches youth that perfection is NOT the goal, but consistent improvement is."

Christopher Childers, youth leader

"There is a shortage of true leadership in today's world. There are many who want power and prestige but evade the responsibility of leading themselves and others. This book is full of actionable ideas and relatable examples that will improve both current and future leaders' abilities to serve those around them."

Ty Draney, coach and educator, Star Valley High School;
thirteen-time Wyoming Coach of the Year

"Chad's extensive experience working with youth as a father, coach, Scout leader, spiritual advisor, and his contributions to other community youth programs show in this motivational book for youth. He showcases his love for youth and his determination to help them succeed and to lead others to success in life by setting attainable goals and by serving others in an inspirational, easy, and positive way. Great for any age!"

Debbie Murri, former volunteer with Chad

"My son asked me to read Chad's book. There were so many things that caught my attention. Wow! This book will be something that I will continue to reference with all my children and the youth I get the opportunity to work with."

Jen Posegate, mother of former lacrosse player

"Coach Chad didn't just coach me; he believed in me, challenged me, and walked with me through some of the most defining moments of my life. Now, as a young adult, I can truly appreciate the depth of emotion and purpose with which he led. Coaches like Chad embody the kind of leadership I hope my own children will one day experience. If you're striving to get 1 percent better today or seeking guidance in leading yourself, your family, or your team, *Change Your Game* is the book for you on and off the field."

Vinny Sliva, former player and former assistant coach

"Coach Chad has made an impact on countless lives in his time as a leader and mentor, including my own. In this book, you will find a guide to help you make that impact yourself and enjoy the rewarding experience of leadership."

Vaughn Ostler, former player and current high school lacrosse coach

"I've looked up to Chad as a leader and mentor since I was young, so it's no surprise that *Change Your Game* reflects the same wisdom, heart, and humility he's always carried. This book speaks directly to young people with encouragement, real talk, and practical tools, and it does it without ever feeling preachy or out of touch. FEED THE WHITE WOLF!"

Jared Tanke, business professional

"This path, this book, is work worth doing."

SGT Jerome Neidhold, former player

"The way that Chad led my youth group changed my outlook on life and inspired me to turn outward and help friends in need. His book captures that same energy and will empower youth to lead and lift their peers."

Alan Cicotte, law student

CHANGE YOUR GAME

www.mascotbooks.com

Change Your Game: Empowering Young Leaders to Ditch Doubt, Find Their Voice, and Impact the World

For more information, please contact:
Mascot Books, an imprint of Amplify Publishing Group
620 Herndon Parkway, Suite 220
Herndon, VA 20170
info@mascotbooks.com

Library of Congress Control Number: 2025916201
CPSIA Code: PRV0925A
ISBN-13: 979-8-89138-801-7

Printed in the United States

J. CHAD MITCHELL

CHANGE YOUR GAME

Empowering **Young Leaders** to Ditch Doubt, Find Their Voice, and **Impact the World**

Dedication

This is not a normal book dedication; it is an interactive one.

I would like you to remember the best teacher, mentor, coach, friend, or compadre you have ever had. Don't skip this. Give it serious thought. Do you have someone in mind? If not, please stop until you do.

Okay, why is the person you chose the best? Is it because they have confidence in you? Probably. Is it because you trust them? Probably. Picture them encouraging you. Listening to you. Smiling at you. Cheering for you. Write here what makes them the best.

I wrote this book to help you in the same way this person did—to help you find confidence and happiness as you recognize your unlimited potential and help others realize theirs as well.

With that person in mind, I hope you will consider this book another great mentor, friend, or teacher.

Now, write the name of the person this book is dedicated to in the blank below. Do this to help you remember this great mentor and thank them for positively influencing your life.

This book is dedicated to ______________________________,
who has been a great inspiration and mentor in YOUR life!

I realize that some of you have never had a helpful, encouraging mentor. That hurts, but it's not your fault. One purpose of this book is to prevent that from happening to any other kid ever again. You can help with that! You can become the encouraging person for others that you never had.

If you fall into this category, let's envision what the best teacher, mentor, coach, friend, or compadre could be like. Think of a wise, experienced, older you, encouraging your present self. The wiser, older you has experienced the challenges and unfairness of life firsthand *and* has learned from them. From that perspective, you see the results of doing hard things and your great potential. The older, wiser you is a familiar, warm, encouraging, and trustworthy mentor. That is what we all need: "Someone who believes in you more than you believe in yourself," as the Boys & Girls Clubs of America says.

So, go ahead and dedicate this book to yourself. Be the greatest inspiration and mentor in your own life!

Contents

Preface

My friend,

I come in hope.

This world is not what I hope it to be. Maybe you're here because you feel this, too.

I hear the complaints and criticisms targeted at younger generations. I don't agree with the haters. I think the opposite. I have great confidence in you, the rising generation of leaders. I have seen you in action. My experiences and relationships with young leaders like you are the source of my hope for a better world.

Hope is power.

In the 1950s, Professor Curt Richter accidentally discovered the tremendous power of hope.[1] The experiment was gruesome. It involved putting rats in jars filled with water to observe how long they could swim before they drowned.

There were thirty-four rats—fierce, aggressive, and known to be great swimmers. How long do you think these rats swam for? Hours? Days? Not even close. Surprisingly, every one of the rats drowned within fifteen minutes of entering the water.

Dr. Richter was puzzled. Why did the rats give up just minutes after being put in the water? He decided to change the experiment with the hope of answering that question. This time, he put the rats in the water for a few minutes, lifted them out, and held them. Then, he repeated the process. Dr. Richter explained that by doing this, the rats learned that their situation wasn't hopeless. Once they had been lifted from the water, the rats didn't give up. Fueled by hope, the next time he left them in the jars, the rats swam for days.[2] Such is the game-changing power of hope.

Here is what *I* hope you will get from this book: Being a leader has the power to change your life and the world for good.

The world needs **you**.

We need principled leaders. We need unselfish leaders. Many of our leaders focus on themselves—their fame, fortune, and what they want. Helping others is an afterthought, if it is a thought at all. This is a double ding for your generation.

Ding 1: You are burdened with the consequences of the selfish choices of prior generations.[3]

Ding 2: You are mired in today's societal momentum of selfishness.

But there's still hope. We can change the game.

In this book, I'm inviting you to participate in a person-by-person, long-game approach to help counteract the damage my generation and the generations before me have done—and continue to do. For that to happen, we need better leaders, and more of them. Leaders like you.

Think about the American Revolution. Opportunity, injustice, and courage combined to lead many hearts to create the foundation for the United States of America. Thomas Paine was one of them. He wrote a short pamphlet called *Common Sense* that was devoured by the colonists in early America. His pen persuaded others to choose liberty and revolution from the chains of the British monarchy.

What is the revolution that we now need? A societal revolution from the chains of greed and factions of destruction. Hearts rebelling against hatred, selfishness, and jealousy. We need wins for the hearts and hopes of society—a fight in which we are currently taking too many *L*s.

We need **you**.

Your family needs your strength. Your community needs your light. Your friends just flat-out need you.

If you choose to lead, your actions, your choices, and your influence can have a stupendous impact that will roll through the world—your world—as a powerful wave of goodness.

You don't believe me? Okay, then keep reading, and we can talk about that.

You don't care? I don't believe that because if you didn't care, you would not be reading this book right now.

Thank you for being here.

We got this. I got you. You'll see. Just stay with me for a bit longer!

Let's go!

—Coach Chad

P.S. Before you start, please scan the QR code and take a quick two-minute survey.

When you finish the book, there is another QR code for a follow-up survey. It's slightly different—just like you will be.

Your responses help us understand growth in mindset and leadership.

Quick. Insightful. Impactful. Thanks for being part of the change.

PART I

Why You Should Be a Leader

I wish that more adults would have talked *with* me, rather than *at* me. This is a void in my youth that I am trying to help fill for you. That's my intent, at least, and I hope it reaches you that way. I'm here to walk the path with you. I'm not pushing you, not pulling you, but am next to you as you try, as you make mistakes, and as you learn from them. I don't have all the answers, or even most of them, but I want to be a trusted friend with some thoughts on leading and why you should believe you can, too. Here goes!

CHAPTER 1

You and Me

"You're making history. The goodness you put into the world creates ripples that never stop. Keep going—your impact is endless."
—Coach Chad

My mom cut my hair for the longest time as a kid. It was so NOT cool. It was big and poofy. My hair was so thick, my friends called it "deer fur"—yikes. I remember when I finally went to the barber to get a "real" haircut. It was so much better. Here were some of my other embarrassing nicknames: Lewis (nerd), Fat Chad (from a football coach), and Chadwick (my least favorite of them all). My favorite nickname: Mitch.

I wish I had had more confidence back then—that I hadn't been so worried about myself. I wish that I hadn't been too scared to say hi to some girls, and I hadn't sounded so dumb. I wish that I had stood up to bullies, and that I hadn't paid so much attention to what *I thought* other kids thought about me—or that zit on my nose, or my clothes, or my hair. Back then, what I wished for was a magical VCR (I guess an app would be the analogy today), so I could rewind my life and do over every dumb or embarrassing thing I did.

I felt the weight of so much pressure from my parents, the community, and myself. There was always the need to be popular, to have friends, and to be cool in the fishbowl society of my middle school and high school. And that was *before* social media!

Part of the reason I wrote this book is to help you cut through the savage amount of garbage that is thrown at young people, so you can get to what matters. My experience (and that of many people who are smarter than me) taught me that direction and confidence in life begin with understanding who you are, your purpose, and what you want to do with the time you have. That was hard for me to see when I was so wrapped up in the drama of adolescence: whether my clothes looked funny, or what so-and-so was thinking about me when I looked at them in the hall between classes.

So, here's a rundown of who I am, and later in the chapter, I will discuss what I see as my purpose.

I come from a large family: three brothers and four sisters. For most of my childhood, the ten of us lived in a three-bedroom house with one bathroom. The boys were in one bedroom, the girls were in another, and our parents were in the last room. Since I was the oldest brother, I slept on the top bunk bed with two brothers in the bottom bunk beneath me, and my youngest brother (nicknamed "Frodo") in the crib in the corner. It was a great, simple life. I played sports, liked to read, had a paper route, fished, and wasn't a very good swimmer, but was good at video games until the simple joystick was replaced by game controllers with way too many buttons, triggers, and colors. By then, my little brothers could constantly kill my character with slappers (meaning the character didn't even have a weapon, and all he could do was slap you) even after giving me the best gun.

Fast-forward to today: I am married to the most selfless person I know. She is awesome. We were high school sweethearts, which was more than thirty years ago. We have six kids (one of whom we fostered and then adopted). We are grandparents, but don't get carried away—I don't sit in a rocking chair or have a walker. Professionally, I was an attorney and then partner at a law firm in downtown Chicago—right on Lake Michigan (think of the TV drama *Suits*—well, kind of). Currently, I am a partner at a law firm in Seattle called Summit Law Group, and I lead it alongside the CEO, Kristin (she is in charge).

I have been working with kids all my life, starting with my seven brothers and sisters. I have coached all kinds of kids' sports ranging from kindergarten to high school age. I have been a leader of the Boy Scouts. I have taken teens canoeing in the Boundary Waters of Minnesota, hiking up Mount St. Helens, and on numerous other trips. My wife and I have led more than 300 teens and adults into the forest for a retreat. I have also led a church congregation of roughly 300 people, including about sixty kids. I have led smaller groups of kids in four different parts of the US: La Grande, Oregon; Orem, Utah; Downers Grove, Illinois (suburban Chicago); and Richland, Washington. My work with kids has been focused on helping them develop mentally, morally, physically, and spiritually (in some instances), as well as mentoring them to be leaders.

The principles of leadership shared with you in this book are what guide me today as a father, a grandfather, a husband, a coach, and a leader at work. I attribute my success in these roles to them for sure!

But that's enough about me. Let's talk about you. I wrote this book for you! Why are you reading it? I don't know the answer to that question. Only you do! But I do know some things about you.

First, we have lots in common. Here are some examples: You can share your story with me, and I can be moved by it—to tears, to anger, to joy, or to happiness. I can share my story with you, and you will find parts that have meaning in your own life. Why is that? Because we are part of the same human family.

What do I know about you? You have a mother who gave birth to you (to quote Glinda, speaking of Elphaba from the musical *Wicked*: "And she had a mother, as so many do." LOL). You get hungry. You poop and pee. You get tired. You can be happy. You can be sad. You have been hurt. You have been excited. You want to be loved and to belong. You have questions. You have desires. You have likes and dislikes. We are both going to die someday. Was I wrong about any of these? Being born and having a body give us a shared experience that allows us the opportunity to relate to and understand one another.

Second, in the same way that you have earthly parents who created your physical body, I believe God created your spirit. I believe in the Supreme Being, the Great Creator, the Almighty, the Eternal One, God, who loves you. But this isn't a book about religion, and you don't have to believe in God to keep reading. I want any person who says, "Yeah, I think I want to be a leader" to be comfortable picking up this book. Yes, I am a follower of Jesus Christ, but I'm not here to push that on you.

What are your guiding principles? If they come from Jesus Christ, great. If it's that you love nature as the Great Creator, and that's what guides you, great! Or if it's that you simply believe in yourself and not in any higher power, great! All your beliefs are welcome.

Bottom line for me: I don't think you have to be any specific type of person for this book to be helpful to you. But for me, my love for Jesus is one reason why I have so much hope in you. You are my brother or sister. I am your brother. We have the same Creator. Our core is goodness. The greatest and most important creation of God is everyone on earth. Our family. This is deeply significant to me and impacts how I see the world and live my life.

Third—and directly flowing from the second point—you have great power and unlimited potential! Do you know the book series and movie *The Lion, the Witch, and the Wardrobe* by C. S. Lewis? Lewis's elevated perspective of your potential is mind-bending. As he explains, there are no ordinary people. We all have the potential to become gods and goddesses, things that, if we saw them in their full potential, we "would be strongly tempted to worship." Believing in your great power and potential is part of the journey to becoming a leader.

Finally, because of your great power, you have great work to do. Why do I think this? Because "with great power, there comes great responsibility" (from the 1962 comic book *Amazing Fantasy #15,* where Stan Lee introduced Spider-Man to the world). But this moral charge is not a twentieth-century invention. One of the earliest references to this principle was from the Prophet Muhammad: "All of you are shepherds and each of you is responsible for his flock." By the way, throughout the book, you will see references to Jesus, the Great Creator, Muhammad, and Buddha. I did this because there is leadership wisdom in their words—all their words.

I cannot tell you what your great power or great responsibility is. Your work will be different from your friends, your parents, and my own. It is yours to discover and do. It won't be easy, instant, or purely self-serving, but it will be worth the effort. It will reward and uplift others and yourself in miraculous ways. As for me? My purpose and great responsibility are to support young people like you on your journey.

Remember: The world is a better place because of YOU!

I hope I might be able to help you in some small way to do your great work.

I am so excited for you and your impact on the world!

CHAPTER 2

Getting the Most Out of This Book

Write in This Book

You **should** write in this book. Underline, highlight, draw pictures, and make notes in the margins or right in the text. If you don't agree with something I say, ~~strike it out!~~ If something resonates with you, highlight or underline it. As you read, ponder, and listen, write down the things you feel impressed to do. There are blank spaces, lined spaces, and dotted spaces throughout the book for you to write, doodle, scribble, or draw. If you're anything like me, you won't do things if you don't write them down, so . . . write them down.

The first section is all about you and why your choice to lead matters—to yourself, your peers, and the world.

The second and third sections are about the do's and don'ts of growing as a leader. At the end of each chapter in those sections, there are three things to help you with the principles we explore:

1. Key Points—Think of them as a handy, quick-reference guide to the takeaways from the chapter.
2. Ponder—Questions to help you analyze the principles you just read about. Think of them like would-you-rather decisions or the options in a Choose Your Own Adventure book.
3. Do—Actions for you to take and apply to *your* leadership principles in life.

Let's explore those last two items (Ponder and Do) some more because they are hugely important.

Ponder 🤔

Bing. Chime. Ding. Clack, Clack, Clack. Buzz. Beep. *So. Many. Distractions.* Can you fight through two things (1) distractions and (2) skimming through this book just to be done? Your best growth and learning will come as you ponder what you are reading.

What does ponder mean? Great question! It means to think deeply. Here are important considerations for pondering or thinking deeply:

- It takes patience and time.
- It requires you to still your mind or, in other words, focus.
- Get rid of distractions. That phone—put it away.

Let's try it right now—honestly ask yourself, What can I do to be a better leader?

"Now listen. Meditate. Examine yourself. And again, listen. You will hear a voice speak to you: the still, small voice of your conscience. You won't hear it in your ear. You will feel it within yourself—deep within yourself—in your heart [or] your mind. It will tell you some things you can do to become a better leader."

This process, laid out in *The 7 Habits of Highly Effective People* by leadership guru Stephen Covey, is an effective way to ponder, and it will make your experience reading this book more impactful.

Do

I recently learned about Bulgarian split squats. If you don't know what that is, it's a type of exercise. You'll need a bench that comes up to your knees or close to that height. Stand about two feet from the bench, facing away from it, with your feet shoulder-width apart. Extend one of your legs backward until your foot is resting on top of the bench. The other foot may move slightly forward, but not much, as you need to find a spot where you are comfortable and balanced. With your shoulders back and core engaged, squat down so your back knee comes close to touching the ground, then return to the starting position. That is a Bulgarian split squat.

The benefits of Bulgarian split squats:

- Strengthens leg muscles (including quadriceps, hamstrings, glutes, and calves).
- Strengthens your core more than regular squats, since you are standing on one leg and working harder to balance.
- Puts less strain on your lower back than traditional squats.
- Allows you to reach a deeper squat, which helps with hip flexibility.

I know what you are thinking: That is great, and I am so happy I *know* about Bulgarian split squats now!

Nope, none of you are thinking that.

You are probably thinking something like (1) Who cares about Monrovian squatty potty or whatever that weird exercise is called? (2) This dude didn't learn about these squats until he was an old man, ha-ha.

We do these in our weight classes all the time. Or (3) I should try that.

These are all legitimate responses. I don't think anyone is rejoicing that they now *know* about Bulgarian split squats, which is good, because simply *knowing* about Bulgarian split squats is not going to do anything for your legs, core, lower back, or hips. Knowing about these squats is not the point, and neither is writing about them, thinking about them, or talking about them. The way to reap the benefits of Bulgarian split squats is to *do* them.

It's the same with the principles and actions we discuss in this book. Reading them is not enough—you won't retain much (if any) of them. Reflecting and writing down your thoughts is better, but it is still not enough. You need to experiment. You need to act. You need to try out the principles for yourself.

"Learning is the consequence of doing," as Simon Sarris wrote. Doing is the path to growth. Oh, and don't worry if you make mistakes along the way. Mistakes are also the path to growth. This is so important that I have a whole chapter on it (chapter 13).

In the next section, we will explore principles foundational to who you are and what makes a good leader: integrity, empathetic listening, appreciating the uniqueness of people, and understanding how your choices and habits lead to predictable results, just to name a few. If you sincerely study this book and apply what you learn from it, your life will change for the better, and you will become a better leader. I have experienced those results in my own life and have seen them in other people's lives. But you need to experience this for yourself. You need to learn for yourself. How is that going to happen? By doing! It is your turn to experiment and see how these principles and ideas work—or don't—for you!

The last section of the book is about potential distractions and hiccups we inevitably face on our leadership journey. Chief among these distractions are what I call the Four "Isms" of the Leadership Apocalypse, social media, and, you guessed it, being afraid to make or admit our mistakes.

Find a Catchphrase (or Hype Meme—Is That a Thing?)

I coach boys' high school lacrosse. One year, we put in a very aggressive defense called a ten-man ride. Sounds funny, huh? It's intense. You take your goalie, who is supposed to be protecting the goal, and have him play defense away from the goal. There are ten players on the lacrosse field, and with this strategy, all ten players (goalie included) are playing defense, which is why it is called a ten-man ride.

We tried to come up with a cooler name for it and were struggling at first. One of the players, Matty, had a "girlfriend" named "Fiona." Here's the thing: I'm not even sure if Matty had a girlfriend, or if her name was Fiona. But that's what the team decided to call our ten-man ride: Fiona. Why did we even need a name for the defense? In lacrosse (like basketball, hockey, and soccer), you can go from being on offense to defense very quickly, meaning most of the time you cannot stop and send in the defense. For our offensive players (now-turned-defensive players) to know what was going on, we needed to have a name for what defense we wanted to run. That name was Fiona. So, when we wanted to run the ten-man ride, one of the coaches or players would yell, "Fiona!" and everyone else on our team would echo, "Fiona!" Then we would go into formation.

That one word triggered so much energy, excitement, and hype for the whole team. I will never forget that code word and the feelings that I still associate with it. Such power in one little word. Even today, "Fiona!" triggers joy.

There is a lesson here. You are going to have highs and lows, including days when it is hard to care about anything, much less being a good leader. That is normal, and it is okay. Sometimes you need a hype word, a walk-in song, a mantra, a slogan, a phrase (or a hype meme?) that you can rely on to take you to a positive, empowering, motivated place.

I have found that music vastly improves my mood and can help me get into a more positive flow. Here are some inspirational songs you might be familiar with:

- Imagine Dragons, "Whatever It Takes."
- Taylor Swift, "22."

I also have my own slogan: Fish On! I hope something similar might be helpful to you, too. Here are a few you might have heard:

- I think I can, I think I can—*The Little Engine That Could.*
- Just do it—Nike.

Toward the end of the book, I'll invite you to choose your own empowering words, phrases, or songs. But I'd like you to start thinking about it now. Whatever you choose, it should fit you, motivate you, and provide you with strength when you are in dire need of a boost or a reminder about why you are doing the hard things. Sometimes it helps if there is a story behind your choice. You probably have a couple of ideas right now. Why don't you write them down, so you'll have a running start when we come back to this later?

Possible catchphrases, mantras, and hype songs

____

____

____

____

____

____

I hope this doesn't feel like a school assignment. I hope you're getting more excited and inspired to become a great leader.

Earlier, I said that I didn't know why you were reading this book, but you did. Will you reflect on this for a few minutes? Your why. Why do you want to be a leader? Why do you care? Why not be selfish and only focus on yourself? Jot down a few notes (or doodles or whatever) about your why. When it starts feeling like a slog, come back to them to get reinspired.

Why I Want to Be a Leader

____

____

____

____

____

____

____

____

____

Squad Work

Another way to approach this leadership journey is to invite one or more of your friends (more than five is probably too many) to join you. Read a chapter each week and then get together and talk about your whys. Share what you liked. Share what you thought was trash. Discuss what you are doing to be a leader.

It might be clear by now that this book is not a quick fix. This is not a read-it-and-forget-it book. We are playing the long game. I hope this book is a trusted friend you keep coming back to—to reread the stories; to look at your highlights, scribbles, drawings, underlines, notes, to-dos, and lists; and to remember what is important to you.

Let's see how you are doing so far:

- Did you write the name of a mentor in the "Dedication" section? If not, stop, grab a pen, and do it.
- Did you write a few notes or sketch something to remind you why you chose that person?
- Can you remember a leader who was not helpful to you? Write some notes here about what makes a bad leader and how you can avoid being one.

We all learn differently. So, maybe you'd rather take a picture of a page of the book and edit it. Or put notes on your phone. Or post on social media and ask your connections about their reactions. Whatever your preferred approach, take a few seconds to log your notes somewhere, anywhere. Approach your experience in a way that excites and inspires you.

Okay, let's see how your greatness can impact your world for good. Fish On! Let's go!

Random Notes, Doodles, and Reflections

CHAPTER 3

What You Do Matters

"If you think you are too small to make a difference, you haven't spent a night with a mosquito."

—African Proverb

Before we dive into principles that will help you understand and do your great work, let's talk about doubts. You know, the ones that the devil sitting on your shoulder[1] may have put into your head. Here's the biggest one we all face at some point: "What I do doesn't matter."

Wrong. You matter. Your choices matter. They are impactful and meaningful. Your choices can influence others and even change the way other people think about themselves. Your choices can be the difference between someone's life and death.

Am I being dramatic? Is that too direct? No. And no. I am not here to give you puppies and lollipops. Life is hard. Life is fragile. You can have more of an impact on someone's life than you may realize. If you still don't believe that, listen to this story (right after the breakout box).

Do you want to know how many times I heard that devil-sitting-on-my-shoulder voice saying, "You can't write this book, no one will publish it, no one will buy it, no one will read it, and you are wasting your time"?

Many, many times.

I heard other messages too that said, "This book is important, it will help others, and it will change the world." I still remember how wonderful it felt when someone who I didn't know very well shared with me how excited they were for my book.

If you doubt that you have greatness to share and that you can change the world, that is normal. But like the little blue fish Dory in *Finding Nemo*, I urge you to "Just keep swimming, just keep swimming." That is what I chose to do and what happened: You are reading this book! That devil sitting on my shoulder's voice was WRONG! So, ignore that negative voice and be like Dory: Just. Keep. Swimming!

When our daughter Chloe decided to move from the West Coast to the East Coast for college, we knew it would be an adventure. Her friends were staying closer to home, but Chloe had chosen to leap out of her comfort zone. It was a bold decision, and like any brave choice, it came with its challenges.

We flew into Charlotte, stayed overnight with friends, and then began the four-hour drive to Virginia. The ride was far from what I imagined. Chloe quietly cried almost the entire way. She was anxious, nervous, and full of doubt, questioning whether she had made the right decision. As parents, it was heartbreaking. We tried to reassure her, but our words didn't seem to land.

Finally, we arrived at her new campus. We were approaching an area where a bunch of college kids were. Suddenly, like a ray of sunshine, a smiling young woman approaches us and says, "Chloe?" It was Lauren, one of the lacrosse players Chloe had met during a campus visit months earlier. Lauren's interaction with Chloe began to change everything. They hugged. They talked. Chloe smiled for the first time that day. (It still brings tears to my eyes even as I write about it many years later.)

That moment impacted everything for Chloe.

Fast-forward four years to a postgame party in Chloe's senior year, when I finally got the chance to share this story with Lauren. I wanted Lauren to know the profound impact she had on Chloe that day.

To my surprise, Lauren didn't even remember the encounter. I couldn't believe it.

This story stays with me because it's a powerful reminder: What you do matters, even if it seems small and insignificant to you. Your small acts of kindness and love have great power.

Can you remember a time when someone did a seemingly small thing that was huge to you? What was it, and how did it change your mood/day/life?

A Small Act of Kindness That Was Huge to Me

I know with all my heart that what you do matters! That means that you matter.

You don't have to be rich, powerful, attractive, popular, White, straight, religious, or whatever to have an impact in this world. If you do something good, if you help others, if you make it so someone feels like they belong, your action matters. The type of leadership we are talking about is leadership by ordinary people—by me, and you, and your peeps. With some desire and a little effort, the opportunities to lead and lift will come. There are many individuals you can impact in extremely meaningful ways if you care enough to lead.

Your daily choices, your small deeds, and your simple acts can and will affect how the world moves forward for centuries to come.

Like the little mosquito that visits you at night—what you do matters!

Random Notes, Doodles, and Reflections

CHAPTER 4

You Have Power— Especially with Your Peers

"A long time ago in a galaxy far, far away . . ."

—George Lucas

Did you recognize this as the "opening crawl" from the *Star Wars* movies? This next story begins a few years after the original *Star Wars* came out, which I am sure you think is a long time ago, like ancient history.

I was in fifth or sixth grade. We had Toughskins jeans, Cabbage Patch dolls, and played computer games with chunky graphics. One day, my classmates and I were asked to answer a question that went something like this: If you had a problem, who at school would you talk to about it?

We later found out that the boy and girl in each classroom whose names were most mentioned would be invited to join a group called "Natural Helpers." The group was an informal peer-to-peer helping network identifying students that kids felt comfortable reaching out to for support.[1] The Natural Helper kids received training to further develop their skills of seeing those in need and helping them out.

Apparently, a few of my classmates identified me in response to the question. When I was invited to be a Natural Helper, I was surprised! I didn't realize that some of my classmates would feel comfortable coming to me with a problem. I was also excited that it would give me a chance to help my friends. I continued as a Natural Helper into middle school and high school.

I realize now that the Natural Helpers were leaders, not because they were the popular kids (though there were some of those), but because they were trusted by their peers and had influence among the different social groups at school.

In fact, the kids who were chosen had two key characteristics: (1) they had the trust of their peers, and (2) they used that trust to positively impact others. Isn't that the essence of leadership? You probably know some kids who meet these criteria. You might already be one of them. Think about that for a moment. Think about the different groups you belong to. Who are the leaders within each of those groups?

The Leaders in the Groups I Belong To

____

____

____

____

____

Natural Helpers were around for many years, but the program eventually died due to a lack of funding. There is a more recent group, however, that uses peer-to-peer relationships for a very cool purpose: Hope Squad, founded by Dr. Gregory Hudnall. In a local high school near Dr. Hudnall, a ninth-grade student tried to give his watch to his best friend. When the best friend refused, the ninth grader replied, "My family would be better off without me." The ninth grader told several friends that he felt like killing himself, and unfortunately, he did. None of his friends ever told an adult. This devastating situation helped Dr. Hudnall see the importance of peer-to-peer interactions and how, with training and guidance, these important relationships could be used to help prevent suicides. Much like Natural Helpers, students at this local high school were invited to name peers who were easy to talk to. After collecting many surveys, the same dozens of names kept coming up. These trusted students were the first Hope Squad members. They were trained to identify suicide warning signs and then connect with adults. For nine years after Hope Squad was implemented in the school district, suicides dropped to zero.[2]

There are more young people in the world today than ever before: 1.8 billion youth ages ten to twenty-four.[3] We read "1.8 billion" and think, "Wow, that is a big number." But it's hard to wrap our heads around just *how* big. Perhaps this will help: One billion seconds is roughly thirty years, so 1.8 billion kids is the same as *the number of seconds in fifty-four years*. That is a lot of seconds, which means that is a lot of young people! In fact, in forty-eight countries, there are more youth than adults.[4]

So, who is going to motivate, inspire, and lead these kids? Who is most up to the task?

You are.

You are best situated to positively influence your peers. And that's not just me talking. That's science.

Many scientific studies have proven what your own experience has shown you: Peer pressure is real.

Take the Chicken Game. In this experiment, test subjects play a video game in which the point is to drive as far as possible without crashing. The further the car goes without crashing, the more points the player gets. You don't control the speed of the car; you just control whether it stops or goes.

The stoplight helps the player determine when a crash may happen. At unknown points along the way, the yellow light appears, then the light turns red. If you choose GO and are successful in getting through the intersection without crashing, you don't lose any time. If you choose GO and crash, you are penalized six seconds. If you choose STOP, that costs you three seconds.

The Chicken Game experiment broke players into three age groups: young teens (thirteen to sixteen), older teens (eighteen to twenty-two), and adults (twenty-four, plus). The players were randomly assigned to play (1) alone, (2) with peers in the same room, or (3) with peers in an adjacent room, with the player knowing that the peers were watching. This experiment attempted to measure how much more risk (i.e., trying to get the best time and thus crashing) players were willing to take based on peer influence.

The Chicken Game showed that when teenagers played a game with their peers watching, they took more chances than they did when they played the game alone. Young teens greatly increased their risk-taking (meaning they crashed more) when their peers were with them, or they knew their peers were watching.[5]

Older teens also increased their risk-taking (though not as much as young teens) when their peers were around. Adults, on the other hand, were not influenced by their peers. One of the experimenters said this about the results of the Chicken Game study: We know that teenagers influence their peers to do things that they may not otherwise do. This study shows that *the mere presence of peers* impacts teens' decision-making.[6]

The second thing science teaches us about why leading your peers is so impactful is the declining influence of parents and other adults on kids. As kids get older, they rely less on their parents for advice and support and more on their friends. I'm sure you can relate. As a parent and former kid, I sure can.

In a survey of roughly ninety thousand US middle school and high school students, less than half of the sixth graders said they would turn to a parent for serious advice, and by senior year that shrinks to only 26 percent.[7] This is true internationally, too. A worldwide survey of nearly three hundred thousand kids aged eleven to fifteen showed that as the youth got older, their parental support dropped, and their peer support stayed almost the same.[8]

Despite the scientific proof and our own experience telling us how much influence kids have on their friends, too many teens overlook peer relationships as a force for good.

Isn't that crazy? It is so crazy. It led me to write this book about your great power as a leader. I am here to proclaim, promote, empower, and help create young leaders. With more young people in the world than ever before, the opportunity for you all to lead each other has never been greater.

Young leaders change the world. The most obvious example is Jesus Christ (Luke 2:42–52). The Bible has been the most popular book in the world for the last fifty years, and the next most popular book, *Quotations from Chairman Mao Tse-tung*, is not even close.[9] Whether these are just stories or events that really happened, billions of people are familiar with the world-changing impact Jesus had in his very short life. His revolutionary (back then) message of love, humility, and acceptance lives on over two thousand years later.

There are more examples of powerful young leaders in the Bible besides Jesus. Think about the story of David and Goliath. As a teenager (though estimates of David's age range from ten to twenty-five) and the youngest of all his brothers, David was anointed to lead (1 Samuel 16:11–13). David volunteered to battle the Philistine giant Goliath when none of the Israelite soldiers or leaders would. The underdog, David, slayed Goliath with his sling and Goliath's own sword (1 Samuel 17).

Another story from the Bible is of Samuel, who served in the temple under the direction of Eli. As Samuel was sleeping, he heard someone call his name, and since he believed that it was Eli calling him, he got up and went to Eli. Samuel did this twice, and twice Eli told Samuel that he did not call him and sent him back to bed. The third time Samuel heard someone call his name, he went to Eli, who figured out that it was the Lord trying to speak to Samuel. Eli told Samuel to answer the Lord the next time he heard the voice: "Speak, for your servant is listening." The next time the Lord called Samuel, they talked, and Samuel was called by the Lord to the work (1 Samuel 3). Samuel was twelve years old.[10]

Some more recent examples of young leaders are Nellie Bly (real name: Elizabeth Jane Cochran), an American investigative journalist who started her career at sixteen years old in the late 1800s. While writing for Joseph Pulitzer's *New York World*, she pretended to suffer from amnesia and delusions so she could get into the Women's Lunatic Asylum on Blackwell's Island. Her report on the asylum's wretched conditions was published in 1887 as "Ten Days in a Mad-House," prompting questions about the treatment of the mentally ill. Nellie would later embark on a solo trip around the world and complete it in seventy-two days! She beat her competitors from other newspapers, and the eighty-day mark set in Jules Verne's novel *Around the World in Eighty Days*.[11]

Gertrude "Trudy" Ederle was another young powerhouse. At fifteen, she set her first world record, and at eighteen, she earned three medals (one gold) at the 1924 Paris Olympics. Trudy's greatest achievement came at twenty years old when she became the first woman to make the thirty-five-mile swim across the English Channel. She beat the men's record by nearly two hours! Trudy's accomplishment destroyed the prevailing view of women as "the weaker sex." She returned home to the largest parade ever for an athlete in New York City, with over two million people in attendance.[12]

Malala Yousafzai is a more recent example of youth leadership. As a child in Pakistan, Malala excelled in school. In 2007, when the Taliban took control of the Swat Valley where she lived, girls were forbidden from attending school. But that did not stop her. When Malala was eleven, she began blogging about her life in the shadow of the Taliban. As she rode the bus home from an exam, a Taliban gunman shot her in the head in retaliation for her advocacy. She was in a coma for ten days and required several surgeries and months of rehabilitation. Still, Malala was not silenced. She and her father created the Malala Fund, advocating for the right of girls around the world to receive an education. In 2014, she received the Nobel Peace Prize for her work.[13]

So, let's review:

✓ There are more young people in the world than ever before.

✓ Young people have a significant influence over their peers—way more than adults have over them.

✓ Young leaders have been changing the world for the good for as long as recorded history.

If you are reading this book, it is likely that you are already leading—whether you know it or not—your friends, other kids your age, and maybe even your little siblings and cousins.

Don't go to the next section yet—sit with this idea for a bit. There are probably many people looking to you for leadership. Let that sink in.

The whole too-young-to-lead nonsense is just that: nonsense that you should not believe at all.

You are NOT too young to lead. You are an immensely powerful being with the ability to lead and create amazing change for yourself, others, and your world.

Later in this book, you are going to hear about one of my former high school lacrosse players and his transformation from a trouble-maker to an invaluable teammate. As I interviewed Brady for this book, I asked him what he wished his coaches would have done to help him that we didn't. You know what he said? I swear on a stack of Bibles this is true: He wished that one of his teammates had stood up and explained to him that this was pulling them all down, that he was hurting the team. As Brady summed it up: "The coaches can do a lot, but the real impact on a player is going to be from the other players."

You might have other doubts that we have not addressed. Even if that is true, have we gained enough momentum for you to keep reading? The opportunity is now. The impact is significant. Your leadership is important. Let's keep going.

Random Notes, Doodles, and Reflections

PART II

Leading Yourself and Others

What is leadership? How can I be a leader? Great questions.

Using your influence to inspire others for good is the essence of leadership. And as we've already discussed, you have influence—with your peers, kids younger than you, and the greater world. Influence is power. Using your influence or power for good is what it means to be a leader.

There are two key pillars of leadership: (1) principles, and (2) doing. It's not six steps. It's not, "Hey, learn these three things." It's a process. A process of discovery, learning, and doing. With different folks. In different situations. In different places. In a different world. With you constantly being a different person.

Next, we'll talk about why principles are important and should guide how we lead. But just talking about things—even important things—is not enough. Think about something you are good at. How did you get good at it? Just by talking about it? By reading about it? No way. It was by doing. Remember how our legs and core get stronger *by doing* Bulgarian split squats, not by *knowing* or reading about Bulgarian split squats? The same goes for leading. We need to do the things we talk about. We need to apply the things we read about. We need to experiment with principles to figure out (1) whether the principle is important or helpful to us and (2) whether doing the principle is something that we are naturally good at or should spend time working on. That is what this section is all about.

CHAPTER 5

Integrity: Do Your Shoes Fit Your Feet?

"If you can maintain your standards and your integrity and you fail, it's okay. It's when you sell out and you fail that you feel pretty sick inside."
—Bonnie Hunt

Think about a pair of shoes that you are dying to have. The shoes are a hot commodity, and you score them via the drop. They arrive, and you do your unboxing. The shoes are crisp, the colors pop, and there is the new out-of-the-box smell. The shoes are better than you imagined. You try them on . . . NOOOOOOOoooooooo! They don't fit. The shoes are too small.

You tell yourself, "I can make them work." So, you wear them to school the next day. At first, the too-small shoes are mostly great. Folks are noticing. They look fresh. The day goes on. Then, there is the pinch in your toes. You can't stop thinking about the nagging wrinkle in your sock at the toe seam. By the end of the day, your feet hurt—badly. Folks can't tell or see anything is wrong (at least at first). They gush about your fresh kicks. But on the inside, you and your feet are not happy.

Life is better when your shoes are crisp *and* fit well—when they look good on the outside *and* feel good on the inside. Like shoes, life is better when it feels as good on the inside as it appears on the outside—when what we believe on the inside fits with what we do outwardly.

In the famous novel *Adventures of Huckleberry Finn* by Mark Twain, the main character, Huck, shares with us the battle raging inside him. Huck struggles to align what he feels inside with his choices. Here's the backstory: Huck Finn has faked his death to escape his abusive father. He then meets and befriends a "runaway slave" named Jim, and the two build a raft to float down the Mississippi River. Jim is caught, and Huck Finn finds out where he is being held captive. Huck struggles with whether he should let the man who had enslaved Jim know where Jim was. At his core, Huck didn't feel right about giving up Jim. After all, Huck "was the best friend old Jim ever had in the world, and the only one he's got now," Jim had told him. On the other hand, Huck believed he was "going to hell" unless he told the slaver where Jim was. In the passage below, Huck describes his efforts to pray that he could tell the slaver where Jim was:

> *I about made up my mind to pray and see if I couldn't try to quit being the kind of a boy I was and be better. So, I kneeled down. But the words wouldn't come. Why wouldn't they? It warn't no use to try and hide it from Him. Nor from ME, neither. I knowed very well why they wouldn't come. It was because my heart warn't right; it was because I warn't square; it was because I was playing double. I*

was letting ON to give up sin, but away inside of me I was holding on to the biggest one of all. I was trying to make my mouth SAY I would do the right thing and the clean thing . . . ; deep down in me I knowed it was a lie, and He knowed it. You can't pray a lie—I found that out.

Sticking to the principle of love for his fellow man, Huck decides not to tell the slaver where Jim is. Instead, he decides "to steal Jim out of slavery."[1]

I love this story. Huck Finn adheres to his inner compass. He can't pray words that are inconsistent with his core beliefs. He is not willing to betray his convictions to try and *live* a lie. Read that paragraph above a few more times, and hopefully, that will pop out. It may help if you think about prayer as doing something, not just saying words.

What the story says to me is that life is better when what we tell others fits with how we feel on the inside. When our shoes look good (on the outside) and feel good (on the inside). In other words, life is better when we have integrity. When our actions, beliefs, and words are aligned. When we are NOT praying a lie.

Think back to Malala Yousafzai. When Malala was shot by a Taliban gunman due to her activism, she continued to advocate for the importance of education. Malala's refusal to be silenced exemplifies having integrity in the face of adversity.

I can think of very few things that upset my kids more than when they catch me being hypocritical—meaning I say one thing and then do another. That will happen from time to time, even when we are doing our best. For example, when I was working on the chapter of this book that talks about empathy and listening (chapter 9), that same night, my wife called me out for not listening to something that one of our kids was trying to tell me. Wow, that hurt! Not that she called me out, but that she was right. My words did not fit my actions. That's a mistake I've made more than once, and I keep on learning from it. I also learn from other people's examples, like Andy Reid.

Andy Reid appears to be one of the most popular coaches in the NFL. One of the main reasons is his integrity. "You can't really listen to a coach or buy into a coach unless you trust everything he's saying," former linebacker Derrick Johnson said. "Andy is a straight shooter. He did everything he told us he would do. That's what everybody loved." Another player said this about Coach Reid: "The things he told us, he did for us."[2]

I believe having integrity is just as important to us as it is to the people we hope to lead. If we want to be true with others, then it is critical that we be true with ourselves. Just like our shoes should fit our feet, our lives should fit who we are.

Do you want to be more secure in yourself? More comfortable in your own skin? Then anchor your actions to what you believe and what is important to you—not what others think of you or their expectations for you. Define your own happiness and do the things that are aligned with your vision of happiness. And by the way, your happiness should look different from my happiness and your parents' vision of happiness. They shouldn't dictate your adult life because you are the one responsible for your own happiness and your own identity. So why do we struggle with integrity?

Lots of reasons, including that none of us is perfect. It can be very hard sometimes. Another reason might be that we don't think we are enough. We don't think we measure up. I have complete confidence in your ability to be a leader with integrity, JUST BY BEING YOURSELF. Some of the greatest leaders I know and have studied were not great leaders because they were popular, had it all together, or never made a mistake. These folks are great leaders because that is what they chose to be. They decided to work on, develop, and do things in a way that was aligned with what they wanted and where they came from. Like Malala Yousafzai, they chose to walk their own path.

Martin Luther King Jr.'s leadership path was rooted in principles of justice and equality. Born into a segregated America, he transformed personal struggles into a mission for change, dedicating himself to nonviolence even in the face of danger. King's leadership drew strength from his identity and experiences as a Black man in America, allowing him to connect deeply with others and inspire collective action. His work—leading the Montgomery bus boycott, the March on Washington, and more—was driven by purpose, perseverance, and a commitment to principles. He taught, "Injustice anywhere is a threat to justice everywhere," emphasizing the interconnectedness of equality.

King's legacy reminds us that leadership is a choice to have integrity and lead with conviction. This kind of principle-based leadership keeps desires and goals in perspective and insecurities in check.

Can you remember a time when you were outside and lost without Google Maps? (Maybe you didn't have your phone with you or didn't have service.) In a situation like this, there are a couple of constants that you can use to get your direction. The sun rises in the east and sets in the west. If you know where the sun is rising or setting, you can orient yourself. Or, at nighttime in the Northern Hemisphere, you can use the North Star to find direction north.

In the Southern Hemisphere, the Southern Cross can point the way south. The rising and setting sun, the North Star, and the Southern Cross are like principles; across time, oceans, and cultures, they are consistent sources of direction and truth.[3] We can follow them to avoid getting lost or confused by loud, glowing voices with no principles, or principles that are inconsistent with our own.

People's needs are the same across time (e.g., shelter and food). The same can be said about our problems. They are generally the same (e.g., greed, illness, and insecurity). The principles we talk about are not flashy new ideas. They have been tried, tested, and proven in various settings across centuries in the forge of people's needs and problems.

Why do we need principles and direction in our lives? Huck Finn needed righteous principles to help him stand against the wickedness of slavery. Alice from the classic *Alice's Adventures in Wonderland* by Lewis Carroll gets this little lesson from the grinning-est Cheshire Cat. While wandering through Wonderland, Alice comes to a fork in the road:

Alice asked the Cheshire Cat, who was
sitting in a tree, "What road do I take?"
The cat asked, "Where do you want to go?"
"I don't know," Alice answered.
"Then," said the cat,
"it really doesn't matter, does it?"[4]

If we don't use principles to guide our direction and actions, then what will guide us? Chance? Our emotions in the moment? Someone else's principles as they whisper in our ear? All of the above? Great leaders don't drift upon winds of emotion or the push and pull of the world. They know where they want to go and understand that principles (when followed) will make their destination more likely to be achieved.

When we operate on principle, we can be more confident and

consistent in our actions and direction. We can use them to chart our own course and to be our North Star. We won't ever be perfectly principled, but we can keep on trying. That alone will make a huge difference in how far we go.

Key Points:

- ✓ Principles are unchanging truths that are important to us.
- ✓ Great leaders use principles to guide what they say and do.
- ✓ Integrity is when your principles, what you know to be true on the inside, fit with what you do and say on the outside.
- ✓ Having integrity is just as important to us as it is to the people we hope to lead.

Ponder 🤔

- Think of a time when someone you know acted with integrity. How did you react?
- Would you rather your friend or a parent react to something you did based on emotion or principle? Why?
- What are some beliefs that resonate with you? Why? One that I liked (that my mom and dad lived by) was work first, then play. When I was young, I hated this approach as my chores stood in the way of what I wanted to do. In reality, I was motivated to get my chores done quickly if I had something to do (play!) afterward. Also, my play was much more enjoyable when I didn't have chores hanging over my head after I was done playing.

Do

- Identify someone you know who has integrity. Compliment them. Ask them how they work to develop integrity.
- Think about someone you look up to. What principles do you think they try to live by? Take one of those principles and apply it to your life tomorrow.
- Think about an issue that you have been grappling with. Is there a principle that you can apply to it, or the circumstances surrounding the issue that will help you work through it? If you think there is, try it! Here is a recent real-life story. Adrian Rodriguez, a California teenager, found a woman's purse in a grocery store parking lot. Adrian could have lived by the belief that "finders keepers" justified a decision to keep the purse and money in it. Instead, Adrian acted on his principle of empathy for others. He considered the woman's potential distress from losing her purse and decided to return it to its owner.[5]
- Did anything come to mind that you felt you should do as you read this section? Did you underline or make a note of something you should do? If so, make a reminder for yourself to do it!

Random Notes, Doodles, and Reflections

CHAPTER 6

Agency: Your Power to Choose

"I was a trembling, because I'd got to decide, forever, betwixt two things, and I knowed it."

—Huckleberry Finn[1]

Who doesn't love a good story that inspires us to be better? A parable is a story that teaches us lessons, mostly about the principles of living a good life. Parables use settings and topics that people can relate to. This is because listeners are more likely to gain insight and understanding if the topics and settings are already familiar to them.

Which parable do you think your friends would find more engaging: one involving social media, or one involving an eight-track tape? Why? Social media will likely be an immediately relatable and important topic for your friends. Eight-track tapes, not so much. Do you even know what an eight-track tape is? Maybe you're googling it now.

You would have to spend a lot of time explaining to your friends what eight-track tapes are before you could even dive into the point of your story.

So, let's explore some parables that teach us about agency, choices, and consequences. Let's start with agency.

On September 11, 2021, I went to the National Museum of African American History and Culture in Washington, DC, and had an experience that I will never forget. The museum tour begins at the bottom of the museum. You start by learning about the history of slavery before the colonies in America. On one wall, there are pictures of slave-trade ships and the harrowing statistics for the countries of their origin:

- France, from 1549 to 1818, transported 1.3 million African captives across the Atlantic to the Americas.
- Great Britain, from 1562 to 1807, transported 3.3 million African captives across the Atlantic to the Americas.
- Portugal, from 1441 to 1836, transported 5.8 million African captives across the Atlantic to the Americas.

On the same wall, there is this quotation from British abolitionist and formerly enslaved person Olaudah Equiano: "We are torn from our country and friends to toil for your luxury and lust of gain."

I was standing in front of the wall, pondering the horrific loss of life and liberty, when I overheard a Black man in a wheelchair speaking to the young lady pushing him. This is the essence of what he said as he was reading and experiencing the same information I had:

"How does God allow this to happen? What could be His purpose in allowing this to happen to so many people? Why? Are you listening to me?"

This last question was directed at the young lady pushing him.

"Yes," she said, "I am listening to you." I was listening to him, too. My soul ached.

You could answer the man's painful questions by invoking the principle of agency. Agency is the power to think, decide, and act for yourself, even when those choices are bad and hurt others.

How important to God is our agency? Important enough to know that many of God's children would be treated inhumanely by others, but to still allow it, like in the case of slavery. Despite people making some horrendous choices with their agency, it is important for us to learn, grow, and become better. Some people also make wonderful choices with their agency.

Agency and choice are closely related. Agency is having the freedom to choose, while choice is what you do with that freedom. Choice happens because of agency.

This next parable, called the Two Wolves, teaches about choice.[2] While its origin is unknown (as is true for many parables), it has at times been cited as a Native American legend. Although it cannot be definitively traced to any authentic source, I'm including an adapted version here because its message is so powerful.

There once was an old Native man. His little grandson often came in the evenings to sit at his knee and ask the many questions that children ask. One day, the grandson came to his grandfather with a look of anger on his face.

Grandfather said, "Come, sit, tell me what has happened today."

The child sat and leaned his chin on his grandfather's knee. Looking up into the wrinkled, nut-brown face and the kind dark eyes, the child's anger turned to quiet tears.

The boy said, "I went to the town today with my father to trade the furs he has collected over the past several months. I was happy to go because Father said that since I had helped him with the trapping, I could get something for myself. Something that I wanted. I was so excited to be in the trading post. I have not been there before. I looked at many things and finally found a metal knife! It was small, but a good size for me, so Father got it for me."

Here, the boy laid his head against his grandfather's knee and became silent. The grandfather softly placed his hand on the boy's raven hair and asked, "And then what happened?"

Without lifting his head, the boy said, "I went outside to wait for Father and to admire my new knife in the sunlight. Some town boys came by and saw me. They got all around me and started saying bad things. They called me dirty and stupid and said that I should not have such a fine knife. The largest of these boys pushed me back, and when I fell over one of the other boys, I dropped my knife, and one of them snatched it up, and they all ran away laughing."

Here, the boy's anger returned. "I hate them. I hate them all!"

The grandfather, with eyes that had seen too much, lifted his grandson's face so his eyes looked into the boy's. He said, "Let me tell you a story.

"I, too, at times, have felt a great hate for those that have taken so much, with no sorrow for what they do. But hate wears you down and does not hurt your enemy. It is like drinking poison and then wishing your enemy would die. I have struggled with these feelings many times. It is as if there are two wolves inside me—one is white and one is red. The White Wolf is good and does no harm. He lives in harmony with all around him and does not take offense when no offense was intended. He will only fight when it is right to do so and in the right way.

"The Red Wolf is full of anger. The littlest thing will spark him into a fit of temper. He fights everyone, all the time, for no reason.

He cannot think because his anger and hate are so great that they consume him. It is helpless anger, for his anger will change nothing. Sometimes it is hard to live with these two wolves inside me, for both seek to dominate my spirit."

The boy looked intently into his grandfather's eyes and asked, "Which one wins, Grandfather?"

The grandfather smiled and said, "The one I feed."

Think of all the choices the young boy made: to buy the knife, to not stab one of the bullies, to be angry at the boys that bullied him, and to talk to his grandfather about it. There is one choice at the heart of the story, though: the choice of the boy to feed the insatiable anger of his Red Wolf or to live in harmony and do no harm by feeding his White Wolf. If the young boy feeds the White Wolf, then he will fuel harmony in his life. If he chooses to feed the Red Wolf, the young boy will fuel anger and destruction. The choice is no different for us—and it's an extremely powerful one.

Cause and effect is the relationship between events: The cause is the action we choose to take, and the effect is the consequence of that choice. For example, if you plant corn seeds and tend to them (soil, water, sunlight), corn will grow, and you will eventually have corn to pick and eat. The planting of and tending to the corn is the cause. The effect is corn growing, so it can be eaten. If you plant corn, will you harvest tomatoes? No. If you plant corn and then do nothing else (no water, no weeding, no fertilizer), will you harvest corn? Probably not. If you eat five Twinkies every day for a month, will you be healthy? No. If you practice piano five days a week for a month, will you be a better piano player? Yes. You practice the piano (a choice), and therefore, you are a better piano player (the consequence). The principle of cause and effect (or action and consequence) helps us understand the power of choice. You can choose your actions, but you can't choose the consequences. The consequences will be the result of your choices—you harvest what you plant.

If you were to tell me what you do every day, every month, over the course of the year, I can get a pretty good sense of who you are, simply because what you do (i.e., your choices) leads to who you are (i.e., consequences). This is the principle of cause and effect: What you focus on and work for, you improve on. If you run all the time, you are a runner. If you build things all the time, you are a builder. And if you make choices and influence your peers to make choices that increase the good in the world . . . you are a leader.

Think of the White Wolf as your Leadership Wolf. If you feed your Leadership Wolf—by being kind, responsible, and an empathetic listener—you are planting seeds of leadership. You are choosing to become a leader, and the consequence is that you will become one. Likewise, if you neglect the Leadership Wolf and feed your Red Wolf—by being rude, apathetic, and unreliable—then you will build upon those negative things!

Brady, one of my former lacrosse players, is a great example of what happens when we choose to feed the White Wolf. Brady had always been passionate about lacrosse, and he had skills. But Brady's attitude held him back. As a freshman, Brady had a me-first, I-know-better-than-everyone attitude.

Our coaches worked with Brady to help him see how his me-first attitude was not helping the team. Brady wanted to be on varsity, so he chose to change. He focused on improving himself each day and each week—just get your mile time better this week. He took things in small bites that were not overwhelming. He also knew he needed to change his attitude and focus on the team instead of himself.

In his junior year, Brady's transformation caught my attention. I remember watching practice from the sidelines and commenting to the other coaches next to me something like: "Wow, is that BRADY?" He was tearing it up. By his senior year, Brady had continued his progression. He was a leader on and off the field. He was also named captain for multiple games during his senior year.

Brady had transformed from an angry, frustrated Red Wolf into a trusted White Wolf of a leader.

Key Points:

- ✓ Parables are stories that help us understand how principles apply to our lives.
- ✓ Agency is having the freedom to choose. Choice is about what you do with that freedom, and consequences are the results of those choices.
- ✓ Who we are is the consequence of our choices, the inner wolf that we feed.
- ✓ Being a leader is a choice you make and have to continually work on.

Ponder 🤔

- What do you do that feeds your White Wolf, the one that prioritizes harmony and doing no harm? What do you do that feeds your Red Wolf, the one with the insatiable appetite for anger and discord? Which of your wolves is bigger, red or white?
- What is your favorite parable? Why?
- What is the most troubling cause and effect in your life? What is a different choice that you can make to have a different

effect? Here are some examples to help you think about this question:

Anger (cause) ➡ unhappiness (effect)

Anger can lead to unhappiness because it keeps you focused on negative feelings, which makes it harder to find peace or joy. When you hang on to anger, it can hurt your relationships and make you frustrated.

Selfishness (cause) ➡ fear (effect)

Selfishness can lead to fear because when we focus only on ourselves, we start worrying about losing what we have or not getting what we want. This fear can grow as we isolate ourselves from others, making it harder to feel secure in our relationships and choices.

Do

- Let's build off one of the Ponder questions above: What is the most troubling cause and effect in your life? Experiment with new choices to see what effect these new choices lead to.
- Do one thing to feed your White Wolf today.
- Make the choice to be a leader.
- Did anything come to mind that you felt you should do as you read this section? Did you underline or make a note of something you should do? If so, make a reminder for yourself to do it!

Random Notes, Doodles, and Reflections

CHAPTER 7

Compounding: Pennies, Snowballs, Habits, and Consequences

"Leadership isn't about big things, it's in the consistent things."

—Drew Dudley[1]

If a genie appeared and gave you this choice, would you choose a penny today that doubled every day for a month (thirty days), or $1 million today?

If you took a single penny and doubled it every day, by day thirty, you would have over $5 million–$5,368,709.12 to be exact. That's the principle of compounding at work. If you changed the time frame from thirty to twenty-seven days, you would have only $671,088.64. This is why compound interest has been called "the eighth wonder of the world. He who understands it—earns it. He who doesn't—pays it."[2]

The principle of compounding is not limited to money. Do

you want to build a snowman? If yes, you need snowflakes—lots of them.[3] You start with a handful. Then, using pressure and energy, you combine your handful of snowflakes with other snowflakes. As you continue to roll the lump of snow, those snowflakes combine with more snowflakes, and those snowflakes combine with more snowflakes, and it just . . . well, snowballs. Keep applying energy and effort, and your snowball continues to grow until it is a solid base for a snowman.

What do compounding pennies and snowballs have to do with you? Compounding is at work in your life, whether you like it or not. Think about this: Improving just a little each day, like 1 percent daily for a year, leads you to become nearly forty times better over that time frame. Go back to the example of practicing the piano that we used earlier. If someone practices each day for a year, they will be a much better piano player at the end of that year. Or, as Michael Jordan said, "If you do the work, you get rewarded. There are no shortcuts in life."

The principle of compounding applies across most areas of life: money, learning, relationships, talents, and work. Getting a little better each day taps you into the growth of compounding consequences.

Compounding reinforces what is happening. Compounding doesn't distinguish between good choices and bad choices. If I keep making the same decision about not caring about what I eat for breakfast (for example, Monday = nothing, Tuesday = root beer, Wednesday = toast, Thursday = nothing, Friday = three donuts and chocolate milk, Saturday = scrambled eggs, Sunday = leftover pizza), those decisions are going to compound. If I care about what I eat for breakfast, those decisions will also compound. You are young, so perhaps your habits do not seem to matter. But with time—think years, not days—your habits' impact on your life can be enormously good or bad.

The choices we make feed our inner wolves. But not all choices are the same. Not all choices compound at the same rate, just like not all snowflakes become snowballs. Some of our choices are more like Takis. Think of these as one-off choices. They are like snacking on little treats. They are more than nothing, but not much. Eating a few Takis here and there (at least for young pups like you all) is not going to make a big difference because you don't eat Takis at every meal (at least I sure hope you don't).

Now, think of your habits and the consistent choices you make that have a great compounding effect. These are like your daily breakfast, lunch, and dinner. What you choose to eat each day during these three meals is going to impact your life significantly: your health, your strength, your looks, your ability to think clearly, to do work, to focus, and to play. The Takis (infrequent random choices) you eat will have a much smaller impact on you. But your habits—whether they are good or bad—are what you feed your wolf for breakfast, lunch, and dinner.

The famed Russian author Leo Tolstoy told a zealous youngster, "Young man, you sweat too much blood for the world; sweat some for yourself first. You cannot make the world better till you are better."[4] In other words, the better a person you are, the better a leader you will be. HELLO? Do you see where this is going, and how important this is?

The better a person you are, the better a leader you will be. The better leader you are, the better your community will be. The better your community is, the better your country will be. The better your country is, the better **our** world will be.

There are great personal benefits too from being a leader, including:

- **Becoming a Respect Magnet:** The positive influence leaders have on others earns them respect. That respect translates into stronger friendships and relationships.

- **Grit:** Leadership teaches resilience. When things get tough, you know how to stay calm and focused, ready to handle whatever comes your way.
- **Standing Out at Work:** Bosses love leaders. If you can guide a team and crush big challenges, you'll be seen as essential.
- **Brighter Future:** Leadership skills make you a top pick for awesome job opportunities. Employers want people who can take charge, influence others to do good work, and make things happen.
- **Confidence Booster:** Leading others builds your self-confidence, which makes it easier to connect with people, earn their respect, and go after your dreams.
- **Master Negotiation Skills:** Leadership challenges sharpen your negotiation skills—handy for everything from school projects to big life decisions.

So . . . let's take a few steps back.

Habits are the compounding of our consistent choices.

What we are is the compounding of our consistent habits.

The better leadership habits we have, the better leaders we will be.

That's the power of compounding.

But this is not a book about habits. If you really want to dive into the subject, the book *Atomic Habits* by James Clear is a great place to start. *For a deeper dive into your habits and how to reset your relationships—including with yourself—I would recommend first reading Stephen Covey's book, *Spiritual Roots of Human Relations*. Here's a powerful quote from the latter book. I hope it gives you a sense of the change you could accomplish in your life just by focusing on your habits.

"Habits have a tremendous gravity pull, more than most realize or would admit. Breaking deeply embedded habitual tendencies, such as procrastination, impatience, criticalness, or living in excesses or selfishness, involves more than a little willpower and a few minor changes in our lives. We're dealing with our basic character structure (what we are inside) and need to achieve some very basic reorientation or transformation, of values and motives as well as practices."[5]

For a crash course on how to develop new habits, use this QR code to access the Bomber Habit worksheet. This was used with our high school lacrosse team right before our season started in spring 2020 (and ended less than two weeks later due to COVID). COVID was a hard reset on life, and I wound up relying heavily on the habit stack I created using this worksheet to help get me through. Those COVID-found habits continue today.

Key Points:

- ✓ Our habits (our consistent choices) feed our inner wolves, for good or ill.
- ✓ Habits are powerful because they have compounding consequences on our lives.
- ✓ Healthy habits (e.g., exercise, empathetic listening, and being trustworthy) make us better people and leaders.
- ✓ Being a great leader has powerful compounding effects on our lives, the lives of those we lead, our communities, and our world.

Ponder 🤔

- What good and bad habits did you learn from your parents? How about your friends?
- What do you think are important habits for great leaders?
- What habits do you think make bad leaders?

Do ⚡

- Make a list of the following: your favorite habits, habits you want to stop, and habits you want to develop.
- Experiment with stopping one of the bad habits and starting one of the good habits every day for a month.
- Complete the Bomber Habits worksheet.
- Did anything come to mind that you felt you should do as you read this section? Did you underline or make a note of something you should do? If so, make a reminder for yourself to do it!

Random Notes, Doodles, and Reflections

CHAPTER 8

Differences and Belonging: No Two of Us Are the Same

"Everyone you will ever meet knows something you don't."

—Bill Nye

After World War II, the US Air Force noticed many pilots were having trouble operating their planes. The theory was that people had grown since the original designs, and it was time for a new cockpit design to fit their larger size. Lt. Gilbert Daniels was given the job of determining an "average pilot size" to help design new cockpits. He came up with ten different body dimensions that he measured and used to calculate the average pilot size. To his surprise, no individual pilots fit the average sizes. Out of the more than 4,000 pilots, none fit the average on all ten dimensions. One pilot had longer arms and shorter legs. Another had smaller hips and a larger chest. Lieutenant Daniels then looked at three of the ten dimensions and found—to his astonishment—that less than 4 percent of the pilots would fit the average on just these three dimensions. Simply put, the average-sized pilot did not exist.[1]

Had the Air Force tried to treat all pilots the same, it would have designed a cockpit that fit none of its pilots. The solution: a cockpit designed with adjustable seats, adjustable foot pedals, adjustable helmet straps, and adjustable flight suits. This concept is now standard in cars; you can adjust the seat, mirrors, steering wheel, seat belt, etc.[2] Because we are not the same, a one-size-fits-all approach rarely works.

It's not just our bodies that make us different; our experiences make us different as well. Let's look at identical twins Conrad and Perry McKinney from New Hampshire. In their early years, they did everything together. They attended the same schools. Both were troublemakers in class. Eventually, their teachers addressed their troublemaking by holding Perry back in fifth grade, while Conrad went on to sixth grade. Conrad graduated from high school, and Perry dropped out. Conrad became a successful businessman; Perry, a homeless alcoholic who slept with trash under a bridge.[3] Later in life, Perry would get sober and become an author.[4]

Let's make this personal. Think about how many different things happen to you each day. Think about how many daily choices you make. What other things make you who you are? Where you go to school. If you go to school. Where you live. What your family looks like. The music you listen to. The books you read. The books you don't read. The social media you see and hear. The things you believe. The thoughts you have. Your feelings. Your emotions. There is absolutely no one like you. Not even close. No one like you has existed before. Your physical appearance, your emotions and beliefs, your personality, your choices, your thoughts, and your experiences make you exclusively unique.

Here is a memorable experience from my life to show how unique we are. We were home during the pandemic, watching a movie with our three youngest kids. It was a Christmas movie about the birth of Jesus. During the middle of the movie, one of our kids stopped the movie and said, "One thing I really like about this story is how Joseph took care of baby Jesus even though Joseph was not his [biological] father." Our son, who made this comment, is adopted.

I had never thought about this before. This new perspective our son shared with us, inspired our family to take care of each other with renewed energy.[5] If we value other people's experiences and perspectives, then our limited experiences and understanding can be expanded.

From India, here is a parable within a parable about different perspectives:

> A number of disciples went to the Buddha and said, "Sir, there are living here in Savatthi many wandering hermits and scholars who indulge in constant dispute, some saying that the world is infinite and eternal, and others that it is finite and not eternal, some saying that the soul dies with the body, and others that it lives on forever, and so forth. What, Sir, would you say concerning them?"
>
> The Buddha answered, "Once upon a time, there was a certain raja who called to his servant and said, 'Come, good fellow, go and gather together in one place all the men of Savatthi who were born blind . . . and show them an elephant.'
>
> 'Very good, sire,' replied the servant, and he did as he was told. He said to the blind men assembled there, 'Here is an elephant,' and to one man he presented the head of the elephant, to another its ears, to another a tusk, to another the trunk, the foot, back, tail, and tuft of the tail, saying to each

one that that was the elephant.

When the blind men had felt the elephant, the raja went to each of them and said to each, 'Well, blind man, have you seen the elephant? Tell me, what sort of thing is an elephant?'

Thereupon, the men who were presented with the head answered, 'Sire, an elephant is like a pot.' And the men who had observed the ear replied, 'An elephant is like a winnowing basket [a flat basket used to sift grain].' Those who had been presented with a tusk said it was a ploughshare [a cutting blade behind the plough]. Those who knew only the trunk said it was a plough; others said the body was a granary [large hut-like structure to store grain made from woven reeds]; the foot, a pillar; the back, a mortar; the tail, a pestle; the tuft of the tail, a brush.

Then they began to quarrel, shouting, 'Yes, it is!' 'No, it is not!' 'An elephant is not that!' 'Yes, it's like that!' and so on, till they came to blows over the matter.

Brethren, the raja was delighted with the scene.

Just so are these preachers and scholars holding various views, blind and unseeing . . . In their ignorance, they are by nature, quarrelsome, wrangling, and disputatious—each maintaining reality is thus and thus."

Then the Exalted One rendered this meaning by uttering this verse of uplift,

"Oh, how they cling and wrangle, some who claim
For the preacher and monk, the honored name!
For quarreling, each to his view they cling.
Such folk see only one side of a thing."[6]

Only by understanding and using the experience of all the blind men could the whole elephant be understood. But let's put the elephant in the corner of the room for a moment (Dad joke FTW). Let's focus on the other part of the story: how our perspective can blind us from someone else's reality. When we are faced with another's different perspective, our pride and ignorance may combine, so we fight, cling to, and wrangle over our perceived truths. This can happen to all of us. Some, however, feed off these differing perspectives for their selfish desires, like maggots.

They are hungry for power and money and champion a perspective that they do not care about, and perhaps don't believe. They take the honest ignorance of the mistaken but good-hearted and whip it into a frenzy of tribalism to make money and gain power. This parable shows us the many-sidedness of things and how we can take our partial experiences as the whole truth. Don't let this part of the parable go unexamined.

I love how author Morgan Housel explained it:

"Your personal experiences make up maybe 0.00000001 percent of what's happened in the world, but maybe 80 percent of how you think the world works. People believe what they've seen happen exponentially more than what they read about has happened to other people, if they read about other people at all. We're all biased to our own personal history. Everyone."[7]

Our different perspectives can be used to sow division, or they can be a huge asset. Great leaders draw upon the unique set of skills and strengths that each of us has. The best leaders find these strengths and help others see how they fit into a team, class, family, or club. This approach helps individuals find success and increases the strength of the team.

Here is one way I learned this lesson:

I was coaching youth football, fifth and sixth graders. We struggled mightily our first year. I don't think we scored a touchdown. It was a great group of kids, parents, and coaches who were all willing to stick through the growth and pain of a tough year. We turned it around in our second year. I remember the first touchdown our team, the West Richland Seahawks, ever scored. It was in the rain, under the lights in Benton City. Oh, the joy on our sidelines after much waiting, work, and frustration. We ended up beating our rival in the semifinal game in overtime—it was one for the ages. We got our butts handed to us in the championship game, but what a season of growth.

That fall, Jon, one of the other coaches, invited me for coffee. Jon didn't know a whole lot about football, but he was so positive with the boys that he kept us coaches charged and focused on being positive with the boys. Jon wanted to tell me that his family was moving to Nebraska. It was a sad day to hear that my friend Jon and his son, Will, who played on our team, were leaving.

I will never forget this part of our conversation. Jon explained to me what a great experience it was for them to be involved in our little Seahawks football experience. And then he told me how important it was that Will felt like such an important part of our team. Jon told me what a great job I did, finding important roles for each of our players to fill. He said that I didn't only help them be successful, but I also helped them understand how their jobs helped the team be successful.

Hearing a dad talk about how important it was for each boy on the team to have a role where they could be successful *and* help the team meant so much to me. Jon also told me how much of an impact it had on our team. For some players, the job that had the most impact was not even on the field during games. Take Will. I don't remember when or how it started, but part of our pregame ritual was for me to say: "Will, get 'em fired up!" Will knew what to do, and he could do it like no other. It was a very *Lord-of-the-Flies*-esque pack of boys jumping up and down, screaming primordially, and getting ready to play ball. He rallied us.

This belonging principle is fundamental to great leadership. Belonging requires a role for everyone to fill.

Key Points:

- ✓ Our different biological makeups, choices, communities, experiences, skills, and perspectives make us unique.
- ✓ Because we are not the same, a one-size-fits-all approach rarely works.
- ✓ Valuing different perspectives is crucial to being a good leader.
- ✓ We can create feelings of belonging when everyone has a role.

Ponder 🤔

- What is the most diverse group you are a part of? Identify three benefits that flow from your differences.
- Identify two people who have had a significant impact on your life. How are they different? How are they the same? Does it matter?
- Think about someone you know who might need your help. Identify an unutilized or underutilized skill or strength of theirs. What's a way that skill or strength can be used to help someone else?

Do

- Make the last Ponder item above happen—help someone see their untapped potential and use it to serve someone else—is there better leadership than THIS?
- Listen to music that you normally would not. Research the artist(s) to figure out what inspires and drives them.
- Strike up a meaningful conversation with a person whose background is different from yours.
- Did anything come to mind that you felt you should do as you read this section? Did you underline or make a note of something you should do? If so, make a reminder for yourself to do it!

Random Notes, Doodles, and Reflections

CHAPTER 9

Empathetic Listening: Or How I Learned About the Power of Pooping

"Be kind, for everyone you meet is fighting a great battle."

—Philo of Alexandria

"Everyone you meet is fighting a great battle." Hard to believe, right? Lots of messages, videos, and posts on IG, Snap, and other social media show folks having the time of their lives and no worries. That is a mirage. There is a lot of pain, hardship, anger, sorrow, and frustration out there.

Roughly two out of three young adults aged eighteen to twenty-five report serious loneliness. Roughly half of these lonely young people said that in the past few weeks, no one had asked them in a genuine and caring way how they were doing. One out of every four young adults surveyed said they have thought about killing themselves in the past month.[1] This is truly serious stuff.

But someone drafted to play in the NBA wouldn't need kindness and friendship, right? Wrong. Even the stars, people we think have everything going for them and are living their dreams, are fighting hard battles and need kindness.

Take former NBA basketball player Travis Mitchell Hansen. He is my cousin and a positive, outgoing person. The same year that LeBron James was drafted number one, Travis was drafted number thirty-seven by the Atlanta Hawks. His NBA career did not last long (but at least long enough for me to see him play in Chicago against the Bulls), and then, he was off to hoop in Spain.

Here is how Travis tells the story of his rough adjustment to life in Spain in his book, *The Next Few Years Will Change Your Life*:

> When I left the Atlanta Hawks to play for Tau in Spain, it was kind of scary. I felt like I wasn't totally in control of things. I didn't know my future coaches, trainers, or teammates. I had no idea what my living arrangements would be like. When I walked out of our townhouse in Provo and headed to the airport for my flight to Spain, I began to cry. I would be traveling far away from my family, and all I could think about was how much I'd miss them. Everything would be new and unknown to me.
>
> When I got to Spain, I didn't know where I was. I didn't have an alarm clock in my hotel room. I didn't even know what time it was. I stayed up most of the first night wondering how I'd make it on time and be prepared for my first day with the team. It was horrible.
>
> That morning, I had my physical examination and

> walked into the gym to get ready for practice. Luis Scola came over to me. He was the best basketball player on my team and probably in all of Europe, and I felt out of place.
>
> "Hey, Travis, I'm so happy to have you on this team. We have heard all about you. If there is anything I can do for you, please tell me and I will do it."
>
> Scola made a great impression on me. He was the nicest, most amazing human being. He . . . was a friend who taught me a great lesson: just be nice to people. It can make such a huge difference. I thought back to my high school days. How big a difference could it have made to others if I would have walked up to them in the cafeteria or in class and introduced myself? If I had just asked how they were doing and made them feel more comfortable? It's such a small thing, but it can go a long way.[2]

Do you remember a time when someone's small act was a gigantic thing for you?

I do. I was a freshman in high school, and the varsity football head coach, Lonnie Pierson, called me by my last name during a summer workout: "Mitchell." Now, he wasn't calling my name off the roll in one of his classes. It was a setting where he didn't need to know my name, but he did! I was hyped. It was such a great feeling to be known by someone I looked up to and wanted to be known by. If there is a time you remember this happening to you, jot down a few notes or doodle about it right here.

A Small Act That Was a Big Deal to Me

____

____

____

____

____

____

____

____

____

____

In the show *Zoey's Extraordinary Playlist,* Zoey (Jane Levy) can hear what other people are feeling. She experiences these inner thoughts and emotions in the form of a musical performance put on by the other person, which only she sees and hears. It feels like a window into their souls. In season two, episode two, a character named George (his voice reminds me of Olaf's from *Frozen*) is being picked on at work by his coworkers. Zoey sticks up for George and tells their coworkers to stop hazing him. George shares with Zoey:

"It's not often that people stick out their necks for one another. Especially for someone they just met. And for me, small acts of kindness like that are gigantic. In my mind, you are a superhero."

The words alone don't do the scene justice. Go watch it. The emotion from George (played by Harvey Guillén) shows how our small acts can be gigantic to others in need.

Zoey, Coach Pierson, and Luis Scola each committed small acts that were monumental for someone else. Why? Who knows? There are likely many reasons. A better question: What small act can you do that will help someone else? Well, you can start by listening empathetically and seeking to understand. It's all part of being a good leader.

1. Empathetic Listening

If there is only one thing you take away from this book, empathetic listening might be the most important one. If Stephen Covey, the great self-help guru of the '80s and '90s with all his experience, research, and knowledge about leadership, treasures empathetic listening, that is a great indicator we should, too:

"Truly, to listen to another with understanding requires a sincere desire plus practice, practice, practice, but it amounts to the richest form of human affirmation and acceptance there is."[3]

Can you see how important it could be to give someone who is fighting a tough battle "the richest form of human affirmation and acceptance"? Great leaders do this! That is a power you can wield as a leader.

What is empathy? It is the ability to identify with or understand another person's motives, feelings, or situation. In the parable *The Master and His Dog*, the dog's foolish owner provides us with **an opposite example** of empathetic listening:

> The dog barked all the night, keeping the burglar away;
> It got a beating for waking the master, next day.
> That night, it slept soundly and did the burglar no harm;
> He burgled; the dog got caned for not raising alarm.[4]

The foolish master hears the dog barking (to keep the burglar away), but the master does not listen to the dog. The master shows no patience or desire to understand the dog. Instead, the master just reacts in anger: "I tried to sleep last night but could not because my bleepity-bleep-bleep dog barked all night."

The master did not value the dog's message and was burgled (robbed). Both suffered: The master was robbed, and the dog was beaten. But what would have happened if the master had listened to the dog and tried to see his dog's perspective? The burglar would have stayed away, the master would not have been robbed, and he would not have caned (beaten) the dog. Win-win.

When we listen empathetically, both the speaker and listener are uplifted. It's a win-win situation. By taking time to listen and comprehend until the other person feels like we understand them, we communicate that we care. We communicate that we respect their experiences and expressions. This gives the speaker a sense of worth and dignity and the listener greater insight. It gives both a deeper connection with each other.

Feeling connected is important. Johann Hari's TED Talk "Everything You Think You Know About Addiction Is Wrong" teaches this masterfully.[5] You should watch it. What does feeling connected *mean*? It means that you know that I am here for you. It means that you know I love you regardless of your choices. What does feeling connected *look* like? It looks like someone is listening to you. It looks like someone understands you. It looks like someone is empathizing with you. What does feeling connected *feel* like? It feels like acceptance. It feels genuine. It feels like "I belong."

Have you ever been surprised that someone knew your name and knew who you were? When Coach Pierson knew my name, he sent me multiple messages:

> I know who you are.
>
> You are important.
>
> You are worthy of my time.
>
> I am here for you.

You can send all these messages to your peeps by being an empathetic listener.

You know that feeling when you are sharing something with a person who is important to you, and they are **not** listening? You were the dog, and the person you were talking to was the foolish master. You know the conversation; it went something like this:

You: Hey, are you listening to me?

Friend [turning to look at you]: Uh, yeah, I am listening to you.

You: Then what did I say?

Friend: You were talking about, uh . . . Sorry, I don't remember what you said . . .

That feels terrible, right? Don't be that guy.

Instead, be an empathetic listener. Do this:

- Put your phone away and give the speaker your undivided attention.
- Whole-body listening—be open (don't cross your arms), face the speaker, look at the speaker, and be mindful of the expression on your face and the rest of your body language.
- Focus on what they are saying, not on how you are going to respond.
- Be mindful of your friend's body language and emotions.
- Listen intently so you can accurately paraphrase what you heard them say.
- Acknowledge you hear them: Nod your head and ask follow-up questions.
- Don't jump straight into fixing the problem. Remember, we are talking about empathetic listening, not empathetic fixing.

But what is the problem with fixing? Isn't that important for us to do as leaders? Sometimes. But more so for ourselves, and less so for others.

When we are great listeners, we express understanding, we show love for the person we are listening to, and we sit with them in their feelings. We experience some of what they are enduring, or at least feel what they feel. When we move from listening to fixing too quickly, we run the risk of:

- Not fully understanding their problem (see more in the next section).
- Focusing more on the problem than the person. Sometimes we try to fix it because the problem and/or feelings the other person is having are negatively impacting us. It's a selfish reason to want to "help" someone. This is what our actions are actually saying to our friend: Your problem is important to me because it is interfering with something I want to do or making me feel a way I do not want to feel. I am not here to listen to you or understand how you feel. I'm here to "fix it" so we can move on, and I can get back to what I want to do.
- Trying to fix a problem that cannot be fixed (or at least that you can't fix).
- Offering fixes too quickly, robbing the friend of their agency. If we take over, the friend doesn't get the opportunity to work through their own problem and arrive at their own answers. Leaders don't undermine others' ability to solve their problems. We support them in making their own choices and coming to their own conclusions.

2. Seeking to Understand

Leaders seek to understand others, not judge them. Judging applies our limited perspective to someone else's situation and distracts us from caring. Understanding helps us care. Maybe a story near and dear to my farts will help.

Have you ever seen a shirt or meme about pooping, perhaps like this?

Figure 1: *Joy!* C. S. Mitchell

I have. And I did NOT get it.

But after a few surgeries and having to take legally prescribed hydrocodone, I learned hydros prevent my body from pooping. It's not like the poop magically disappears. It gets stuck like a log jam. It does not move. That can't last forever. Something has to give. If you have never sat on the toilet for five hours, contemplating whether you should call 911, and finally deciding to use suppositories filled with nitroglycerin to get things moving, then you really cannot relate, right?

Having lived that experience twice (I know, I know, sometimes I have to make the same mistake multiple times before I learn my lesson), I *now* understand why folks get excited about pooping! In my young life, I had taken for granted many, many times pooping with ease. But now, I have some understanding of another side of pooping—not being able to. I get the joy of having the log jam finally move along. I understand more than ever (and at least from my own experience, I am sure there are millions of other legitimate reasons why folks get excited about pooping).

Why is understanding others and their experiences important?

"We must first seek to understand others as they understand themselves, to see the world through their eyes, to stand in their shoes, that we may understand why they behave as they do."[6] Another great quote from Stephen Covey from his book *Spiritual Roots of Human Relations*.

Judging is the opposite of understanding. Judging is taking *my* experiences, feelings, understanding, and perception, and attributing them to another person's situation. This was me judging:

> Look at that dumb T-shirt that person is wearing. The T-shirt says, "I pooped today." What a dork. We all pooped today, big deal. I am not going to celebrate my personal bathroom life with others. Plus, there's nothing to celebrate. Everyone poops!

I judged that person hard until life gifted me with a different perspective: Not being able to poop for days on end and thinking about having a bunch of paramedics come to my house to help me get off the toilet. I labeled the person a "dork." I talked about them being silly. My conclusions came from my own limited experiences, feelings, and understanding.

Okay, so let's step away from the toilet and get to the point.

When we judge someone, our focus is on what the person is doing and what it says about them: lying—so they are a liar; being mean—so they are a bully. Judging focuses on *what* they are. Our conclusions may be based on our limited understanding. Remember the parable of the blind men and the elephant? Each man described what the elephant was based on their limited experience with the elephant.

When we seek to understand, our focus becomes on *how* the person is doing in the moment. For example, when I am being rude to someone and my kids see it, some of them are very good at focusing on *how I am*. It can be as simple as the following:

Me: (acting rude).

Son: Hey, Dad, what's up?

Me: Nothing.

Son: Well, you were rude to that person, and that is not like you. How are you doing?

Me: Fine. (pondering for a moment) I guess I am stressed out about work.

Son: Ah, what is going on at work?

Empathetic listening and seeking to understand help us focus on the person behind the behavior. And it can lead us to the small act that can help them through whatever hard battle they are facing in the moment.

Key Points:

- ✓ If you assume everyone is fighting a hard battle, you will likely be right.
- ✓ There are little things you can do to help others, which can be a huge help to them.
- ✓ Great leaders are empathetic listeners.
- ✓ Leaders seek to understand others, not judge them.

Ponder 🤔

- What little thing has had a significant impact on your life?
- How well do you listen to others? How can you improve your listening skills?
- Who do you know who is an empathetic listener? What makes them an empathetic listener? What can you learn from this person to be a more empathetic listener?

Do ⚡

- In the next two minutes, do something small for someone that you believe will positively impact them.
- Text or DM someone who did something nice for you to let them know what they did helped you!
- In a mirror or using your phone, practice what it looks like when you are listening empathetically.
- Did anything come to mind that you felt you should do as you read this section? Did you underline or make a note of something you should do? If so, make a reminder for yourself to do it!

Random Notes, Doodles, and Reflections

CHAPTER 10

Being the Light: Choosing Team Sun or Team Shade

"Shade never made anybody less gay."
—Taylor Swift

My family is full of Swifties. I hear her music a lot. The lyrics above are from the song "You Need to Calm Down," which have really stuck with me. I don't think I have ever seen a person positively influenced by someone else throwing shade at them. Have you?

The person who was shaded might have been embarrassed and, in that moment, stopped something they were doing or saying . . . but in terms of shade equaling positive change, I don't think it happens. Trying to help others is not the reason people throw shade to begin with, right? It is usually to try to make themselves feel better by putting someone else down—to pick a fight, or to hurt someone. They do it to make someone else feel bad, because the shade-tosser is feeling bad and doesn't want to be alone in those feelings.

One winter, on a bright Saturday morning, our dog Barley and I were out walking. It was one of those mornings where it was nice and warm when you walked in the sunshine, but when you walked in the shade cast by a tree or house, it was a bit chilly. As we walked past one house, I noticed a cold, white-frosted spot on the roof. Every other part of the roof was black and warm with the sun shining on it. Then, I noticed an old scraggly tree was growing near the house. The gnarly tree stood between the sun and the roof and cast a shadow on the roof that prevented the warm, bright sun rays from melting away the early-morning frost.

As we continued to walk, I realized I needed to share this parable with you. Are you Team Sun or Team Shade? Do you lift others with your words and make them feel good (Team Sun)? Or do you judge others and criticize (Team Shade)? Do you serve others (Team Sun)? Or do you manipulate others for your benefit (Team Shade)?

Who are the more capable leaders, the folks on Team Sun or Team Shade? Team Sun feeds your White Wolf. Team Shade feeds your Red Wolf. When you choose Team Sun, you choose to be the kind of leader our world needs more of. Make a choice right now that will have an awesome impact on other people: Choose Team Sun!

But let's acknowledge that it's hard to be on Team Sun all the time. Sometimes life is a drag—you are likely fighting your own hard battles. Sometimes things don't go our way. Sometimes our emotions overcome us, and we lash out. Sometimes we are targeted by Team Shade. We can't always be the light that someone needs. But we can try to never be Team Shade (and when we do make a mistake and throw some shade, we can recognize and apologize—see "Chapter 13:

Mistakes Are Part of the Journey").

How can we make it easier not to be on Team Shade? Fred Rogers, the star of the show I grew up watching, *Mister Rogers' Neighborhood*, carried around in his pocket a quotation that read, "Frankly, there isn't anyone you couldn't learn to love once you've heard their story." In other words, look for the good in others, and you will find it! What can help us find the good in others? We've discussed many of the things that can help: listening empathetically, seeking to understand, and respecting different experiences and perspectives. We can choose empathy, warmth, and understanding. Or we can choose to add hate and negativity to the pile, offering more weight to an already heavy load.

The only way Team Sun can be limited is by hate and selfishness. Many people in this world choose these things. They choose to limit love for themselves and what they give to others. But they don't have the power to limit the love that you have for yourself or the love that you can give to others. Team Shade can certainly make it harder for us to love (it is easy to love your friends, much more so than your enemies), but we still have that choice.

I cannot talk about Team Sun without talking about Jesus Christ. After Christ's resurrection from the dead, Jesus asked Peter (the person in charge in Christ's absence) three times, "Lovest thou me?" Each time Peter's reply was the same: "Thou knowest that I love thee." Jesus responded to Peter, "Feed my lambs . . . Feed my sheep . . . Feed my sheep" (John 21:15–17). Once Christ was gone, Christ wanted Peter to do the loving, caring things He did. That is Team Sun. Christ wants us all taken care of. He wants us to be fed. He wants us to be tended to. He wants us to be safe. He wants us to be in his fold. He wants us to know the truth, and He wants us to have joy. We are all much happier when we are fed and taken care of, and when we know someone is serving us and loving us through that service. That is the way Christ lived and died.

Jesus taught that there is no greater love a person can have than to lay down their life for their friends (John 15:13). I have mostly thought of this as dying for our friends—literally taking a bullet for them. That could happen, but it's not very likely. What is more likely is having opportunities, every day, to put our friends' needs before our own. To spread sunshine.

Every time I watch the music video for Andra Day's "Rise Up," I get choked up. If you have not watched it, you need to.[1] Be ready to get in your feelings from that song and video! Little things each day. The courage and unselfishness the young lady shows to her partner by helping him get ready for their date. The commitment of the wounded marine who chooses life and living, even though his life has been impacted and changed forever in a devastating way. These are heroes. These are leaders. They are leading themselves, and that allows them to lead others. Showing leadership through example and service to others is so much louder than words! SO MUCH LOUDER THAN WORDS!

Service to others shows a commitment and love that is deep and devoted. I believe this is what Christ wanted Peter to do every day. For all the sheep. For all of us. Over. And over. And over again. Do you want to know the pinnacle of great leadership? This is it! Great leaders serve others because they care about them. And like the young lady in the video shows us, you do it every day, and you will "do it a thousand times again."[2]

What is the cost of leadership? It's self-interest.[3] Selfishness. As the Prophet Muhammad taught, "The best of humans are those who are most beneficial to others."[4]

The greatest leaders put others' needs before their own. They are selfless. They serve. They are patient. They seek to understand. They are loving. We can be that type of leader. And we can do it every day—at least we can try to. We are human, and we will make mistakes, but getting back up to try again is great leadership.

We don't need titles. We don't need authority. We don't need permission. We don't need a certificate or degree. We just need to choose. We need to feed the White Wolf. We need to choose Team Sun. We need to listen to others. We need to shine a light on them, not shade them. People don't want our judgment. They need our love. We cannot effectively offer them both.

"What is the finest expression of the law of love?" Stephen Covey asks in his book *Spiritual Roots of Human Relations*. "To accept and respect another person, in all his uniqueness, just as he is, which includes what he may become."[5]

When we see others with this light, we can lead with our light.

One of the great things about Team Sun (have you figured out that Team Sun = love?) is that it is not a zero-sum game. Meaning, it is unlimited. It's not like Bitcoin, where there are only so many Bitcoins in the world, and if I have eight of them, those are eight that someone else cannot have. Love is infinite. If I give some of my love away, I have lost nothing. It's not like food: I gave you my apple, now I don't have an apple to eat.

In fact, I think it works in reverse: I give love, you get love, and now we both have love, which creates more love in me, more love in you, and encourages us to give more love. The Buddha teaches, "Thousands of candles can be lighted from a single candle, and the life of the candle will not be shortened. Happiness never decreases by being shared." And I would add, leading others with love and encouragement sets in motion endless ripples of good. Those ripples impact everything around us.

Here's my own story that proves the multiplying effect of love: We had moved to a new area. I got to church a little early, and an elderly lady was sitting in the back by herself. I felt prompted to introduce myself to her. I did and asked if I could sit next to her. Her face lit up immediately, and that small, simple moment became the start of something much bigger.

Her name was Sharon, and as we talked, I learned she was kind, funny, and full of stories. She later told me how much it meant to her that someone took the time to sit by her and get to know her. This was the beginning of a great friendship. To Sharon, my simple act of introducing myself to her, sitting by her, and getting to know her better was gracious. Now, whenever she sees me, she expresses kindness back to me.

What I didn't expect was how much Sharon's warmth would come back to bless *me*. Over time, she became one of my greatest supporters. When she would see me, her face would light up, and she'd go out of her way to encourage me or ask how I was doing. Her warmth and joy made me feel seen and valued, especially during times when I truly needed it.

Looking back, I realized that one small act—saying hello and sitting with her—created a ripple effect. It didn't just make Sharon feel good in that moment; it grew into a friendship that has brought joy to both of us. Team Sun works like that—it multiplies.

Key Points:

- ✓ Being on Team Sun is not a zero-sum game. Love never decreases by being shared.

- ✓ We can't always be the light that someone needs. But we can commit to never being Team Shade.
- ✓ People don't want our judgment. They need our love. We cannot effectively offer them both.
- ✓ Great leaders are motivated by love for those they serve.

Ponder 🤔

- Who has shown me love in a way that makes me better? How?
- Have you heard the saying, "Hurt people, hurt people"? Does this make sense to you? How can knowing this make you a better leader?
- What is one step you can take to move toward Team Sun?

Do ⚡

- Commit to taking that one step that you thought about to move toward Team Sun.
- Find a quiet, private place for you to answer one of these questions: What keeps me from loving more people? Or, what keeps me from loving my friends more fully?
- Write in your journal three things you love about yourself! If you have made it this far in the book, here are two that I think are true and worthy of loving yourself: (1) you want to do better, and (2) you are a leader!
- Did anything come to mind that you felt you should do as you read this section? Did you underline or make a note of something you should do? If so, make a reminder for yourself to do it!

Random Notes, Doodles, and Reflections

PART III

Barriers to Being a Leader

Just like there are many principles to help us be better leaders, there are countless distractions and hurdles along that path. Let's know these enemies so we can more effectively deal with them.

CHAPTER 11

The Four "Isms" of the Leadership Apocalypse

"If you know the enemy and know yourself, you need not fear the result of a hundred battles."

—Sun Tzu, *The Art of War*

"Isms" are three letters you can add to the end of some words to make them refer to an oppressive and discriminatory attitude.[1] "Isms" judge or discriminate based on a specific quality. At their core, "isms" are driven by selfishness and fear.

We are going to explore what I think of as The Four "Isms" of the Leadership Apocalypse: Tribalism, Racism, Sexism, and Materialism.

Tribalism = treating a tribe/group as inferior or the enemy because they are not your tribe/group.

Racism = treating people as inferior based on their race.

Sexism = treating people as inferior based on their sex.

Materialism = treating people as inferior to material things (e.g., money, cars, or lifestyle).

1. Tribalism

If you have followed politics in the US, you have seen tribalism in action. If you are a Democrat, then some folks think that means you are an un-American socialist, and that is bad. All other kinds of judgments flow from those beliefs. On the flip side, if you are a Republican, then some folks think you are an un-American fascist, which is bad. And all other kinds of judgments flow from those beliefs.

The benefit both sides experience by spewing this hatred is that it helps garner power, money, and energy to defeat the opposing party. The higher the stakes—"Our country and our freedoms are at stake!"—the more you may hate and demonize the other side and give more $$$. Fear is the engine of tribalism: forming tribes, funding tribes, and keeping the tribes fired up. Most "isms" are a form of tribalism: Blacks vs. Whites, Men vs. Women. One of the most effective tools used to manipulate others is creating an "us-against-them" narrative.

Tribalism was rampant when I was in high school, and I still see it as a coach. When I was a teenager, I was enveloped by it. Folks at my school did not like certain schools that we played each year in multiple sports. And forget about dating someone from a rival school—that just couldn't happen. They were the bad guys, and we were clearly the good guys. We got into fights, in and outside of sports, which just added fuel to the fire. We did not start the tribalism—we grew up in it—but we continued it.

My perspective changed when I graduated, and I got to know players from other schools. A few of my teammates and I played in an all-state game and got to know some of the players from our rivals. Guess what? These were some cool people. I had the same experience playing football in college: Some of the guys on the team were from our rival high schools. Guess what? We became friends. They were good guys! Once I got out of the tribal atmosphere and spent time with these people, I realized that beneath the different colored jerseys, they were a lot like me.

Tribalism is particularly powerful because it can blind us to the truth. When people get information that is consistent with their tribal beliefs, they are willing to accept it with little investigation. And you can guess what happens with information that is inconsistent with tribal beliefs: It is easily pooh-poohed regardless of the source.[2] In high school, tribalism blinded me to the truth that folks from other schools were good people. The tribalism of our high school rivalries blinded me to some other fundamental truths:

- Stereotyping an entire school (or any group of people) is foolish.
- The kids at the rival high schools were fighting hard battles just like the kids at my school.
- I could choose to get out of the tribal mentality.
- Understanding, empathy, and love can tear down long-ago-built tribal boundaries.

You might be saying, "Chad, wait. A tribe sounds a lot like that feeling of being connected you talked about, which you said was very important." True. A tribe is based on connectedness. You belong to your tribe, your group. The problem with tribalism is not that you are connected; it is what's connecting you and what your purpose is being in that tribe.

Let's go back to rivalries. There is nothing wrong with having school pride. The connection you feel with your school is a good thing. The problem occurs when you look at your school relative to another and hate that other school, demonize it, or treat it as the enemy. Like many things, you need to look at the why. Are you connecting with people for good? That is, belonging. Are you connecting with people to belittle, demean, or harm others? That is tribalism. The upside to any tribalism is that you can grow out of it.

2. Racism

In some ways, racism is simple to understand and reject because it is so blatant and obviously evil. Most people believe that police officers using excessive force and killing George Floyd, an unarmed Black man, was horrific. In fact, millions of people of all colors and races were so horrified by this blatant and fatal act of racism that it sparked protests across America and in over sixty countries in support of the Black Lives Matter movement—in the middle of a once-in-a-century pandemic.

But in other ways, racism is subtle.

It was our senior year in high school. We had a football jamboree against one of our rival teams at their place, and someone had the idea of us sharing watermelon after the jamboree. That didn't go as planned, and we mostly took the watermelon, got on the bus, and left. Somehow, I ended up with a whole watermelon. I was not sure what to do with it. We had already eaten some, so I didn't want to crack another open. I thought it would be funny to put it in my buddy Anthony's locker.

The next day, I went to get into my football locker. Some of my other teammates, not Anthony, had taken the watermelon I put in

Anthony's locker and had done their best to force the entire watermelon into my locker by grating it on the locker door. The lockers were made of a solid, thick metal that looked like an oversized cheese grater. It looked like someone had blown watermelon puke into my locker. Pink. Sticky. A mess. When I saw this, I was so confused. What happened? Why did some of my teammates do this?

They were sticking up for my friend, whom I had been racist toward.

Anthony is Black. I am White. Anthony was one of my best friends in high school. We lifted weights in the offseason. I was a groomsman at his wedding. Many years later, we still keep in touch. But there is a racist stereotype that Black people love watermelon, and my putting the watermelon in his locker fed into it.[3]

My head was spinning. I talked to Anthony. He mostly shrugged it off. I explained to him that I didn't mean to hurt his feelings, and he believed me. This experience has stuck with me. Anthony was my friend, and I didn't mean to hurt his feelings; it was supposed to be funny. But what was funny to me, and my experiences, was very offensive to others with different experiences, understanding, and perspectives.

Racism can exist anywhere. Our experiences, or upbringing, can perpetuate racism. This was my opportunity to listen, seek understanding, learn from my mistakes, and grow.

The pull of racism can be powerful. In 1919, the Fairground Park pool in St. Louis was the largest public pool in the US. It was huge (enough room for up to ten thousand swimmers), had a sand beach, and a fancy diving board. It was for Whites only. Then, civil rights leaders in the 1960s successfully pushed for public pools to be integrated. You'd think this was a positive thing, right?

After forced integration, however, the Fairground Park pool was drained and closed for good. I can just hear folks from that era saying, "I would rather have no pool than have to share a pool with n*******." Shocking? That was the mindset. The closure hurt Black people. The closure hurt White people. No one could use the pool anymore.[4] How destructive.

I once saw a viral video of a White lady yelling at Black people, "I am going to teach my grandchildren to hate you!" How sad. How ignorant. How pathetic that the lens some people choose to see through is one of race. "If you are White, you are okay. If you are Brown, I don't want to be around you." Think of the stories, lies, and trash they have to believe to see a Black, an Asian, or a Latino person and see evil or something less than human. What does that say about how the racist is living his or her life? What does that say about the racist's view of humanity? What does that say about their future? Their happiness? Think about the damage that does to someone's integrity and identity.

As we work to listen and understand, these principles apply across the board: to the person who is discriminated against and the racist.

3. Sexism

The most common form of sexism is misogyny, meaning hatred of, contempt for, or prejudice against women. What can misogyny look like? In its most extreme forms: violence, slavery, sex trafficking, and rape. It can involve treating women as objects or as less than human. Sexism has its roots in a lack of respect and a desire for control. Take, for example, the sexual harassment of women. Data shows that it is mostly motivated by a desire for power over women. "The problem is not self-control. It's a culture that normalizes control over women,"

Adam Grant, best-selling author and professor of organizational psychology, has stated.[5]

It seems there are high-profile cases of some men's despicable behavior against women in the news every day. These obvious examples of toxic and sexist behavior are easily seen as wrong. But like racism, sexism can also be more subtle and difficult to identify.

One less pernicious form of sexist behavior is labeling the same conduct differently based on sex. Women are bossy, but men are assertive. Women are emotional, but men are passionate. Expectations based on sex are also sexist: Women are supposed to be kind and helpful. Men are meant to be driven and powerful. Women's jobs are to clean and cook. Men's jobs are to be leaders and take charge.

Do you see the problem with sexism? It ignores agency. It projects certain beliefs onto an entire population based merely on sex, ignoring our individuality and differences. Some women want to stay home and not have a career. Some men want the same thing. Some men wear their emotions on their sleeves. Some women like to hunt and fish.

The two most influential human relationships in my life are with women: my mom and my wife. I love them. They are very different. I respect them. I want them to be respected by others. They deserve it.

4. Materialism

In places where monkeys swing from trees, there are tales of monkey traps. A shiny thing is put in a coconut or jar, which is then tied to a tree. The shiny thing's flash and glitter grab the monkey's attention. The hole in the top of the jar is just the right size. The monkey reaches into the jar to grab the shiny thing. Reaching into the jar with an empty hand is not a problem for the monkey, but when the monkey grabs the object, the monkey's hand creates a fist. The monkey's hand is now larger than the hole in the jar. The monkey cannot pull its hand back out of the jar unless it lets go of the object. Instead of letting go of the shiny thing and breaking free, the monkey hangs on to it and is trapped until the trapper comes and takes the monkey away.

Figure 2: *Stuck Monkey in Tree*, C. S. Mitchell

This last "ism" is materialism: being occupied with things and what you believe they do for your social image. Materialism values things over people, but don't be fooled—materialism is not limited to rich folks. It afflicts the rich and poor alike. Whether the monkey is wealthy or poor is not the problem; the problem is that the monkey is so fixated on the shiny thing that it is entirely distracted from its own well-being—not to mention the well-being of its family and friends.

I got caught up in materialism in middle school. I was lucky to have made the school basketball team. Our team colors were blue and white. Once I made the team, my dad took me out to buy shoes. Most of the cool guys on the team were buying "Weapons" shoes, made famous by Earvin "Magic" Johnson (LA Lakers) and Larry

Bird (Boston Celtics). There was also a cool pair of shoes made by a newer company and worn by one of the younger NBA players: Michael Jordan. But his shoes' colors didn't match the colors of our school uniforms. Jordan played for the Chicago Bulls, so his shoes were red, white, and black. Well, I could not afford Air Jordans or Weapons, so I got shoes that looked a lot like Air Jordans, but not Nikes. I guess I learned about branding and materialism. I recall being embarrassed that my shoes were knock-offs.

Figure 3: *Jordan Wannabees*, C. S. Mitchell

Materialism is a two-horned monster:

- Horn one: Materialism turns us away from others to focus on ourselves. *Are people paying attention to me? What do these sneakers say about me?*
- Horn two: Materialism forces us to compare ourselves to others. *How can I be happy with two pairs of Dunks when Trey has three, and one of them is the Ben & Jerry's Chunky Dunk collab?*

When he was seven or eight, our youngest was obsessed with comparing his chores, bedtime, and things to his older brother's. He was relentless, always attacking whatever difference there was between him and his brother: Why do I have to go to bed now, and Quinn doesn't have to? Why do I have to pick up all the poop in the backyard from the dog and Quinn only has to unload the dishwasher? Our message was not getting through, so his mom sat him down and made him write out many times:

Comparison is the thief of joy.

Comparison is the thief of joy.

Comparison is the thief of joy.

Comparison is the thief of joy.

After memorizing this phrase and naming the feeling (jealousy) when it happened, it helped our son notice when he was doing the comparison thing and then work on controlling it.

The race for more (more money, more stuff, more followers) is a race that cannot be won. There will always be someone with more. The results are unhappiness and undue stress. Research shows that our lust for things and status can lead to anxiety, depression, broken relationships, and a lack of empathy. In one study, eighteen-year-olds were asked to rank by importance to them jobs, money, and status on the one side and self-acceptance and feelings of belonging on the other. They were also tested to identify mental health problems. Then, they were asked the same questions twelve years later. At the ages of eighteen and thirty, materialistic people were more susceptible to mental health disorders. Importantly, the folks who became less interested in jobs, money, and status over the twelve-year period also reported fewer mental health issues.[6]

Another study looked at 2,500 people for six years and found a connection between materialism and loneliness. The results showed that materialism led to social isolation, and similarly, isolation led to materialism. People were substituting human connection with possessions.[7]

Yet another study put a group of teens through a program designed to steer children away from spending and toward sharing and saving. The self-esteem of materialistic children in the program rose significantly as they learned these crucial life skills. Those who had little interest in materialism before the program experienced no change in self-esteem.[8]

How good a leader can you be if you are stuck with your hand in the jar, hanging on to something flashy and exciting—the new thing that everyone wants? Where is your focus? Is it so much on the shiny object that you sacrifice your own well-being? How can you expect to grow if you can't even take care of yourself? How are you going to effectively serve or lead others when you cannot lead yourself?

There are two important perspectives we can use to beat back the two-horned materialism monster: put things in proper perspective (value people over things) and love (serve people, let go of that shiny object so you can

Antidotes to Isms

What are antidotes to "isms"? At least three of the principles we've already explored can help us combat The Four "Isms" of the Leadership Apocalypse.

1. Everyone is different, so stop trying to corral people into groups and stereotypes.
2. Empathetic listening and not judging (here specifically based on group, race, sex, or material wealth).

3. Love. If we can hear a person's individual story, we can find a way to love them for who they are instead of seeing them as less than or "other."

Perhaps you will want to go back to section two to find the principles that will be your antidotes to The Four "Isms." Remember, growth is always an option that we can choose. And if we make a mistake, we can choose to make amends and learn from the experience. I have certainly learned a lot about my own need for integrity and growth regarding my racist, sexist, materialistic, and tribal beliefs.

Key Points:

- ✓ Fear and selfishness are the root of The Four "Isms": tribalism, racism, sexism, and materialism.
- ✓ Are you connecting with people for good? That is belonging. Are you connecting with people to belittle, demean, or harm others? That is an "ism."
- ✓ Leaders need to understand their weaknesses and challenges, including working to combat each of the "isms" in themselves and society.
- ✓ Recognizing and appreciating differences, listening empathetically to others' stories, and loving and serving others are great ways to combat all the "isms."

Ponder 🤔

- How have "isms" impacted you?
- What tribes do you belong to? Where is tribalism used to treat others as inferior in your life?
- Are you sometimes sexist, racist, or materialistic? How about

the people you hang out with? Are they a good influence on you with respect to these "isms"?

Do

- Read a book that will help you better understand the devastation and long-lasting effects of slavery. For example, *Twelve Years a Slave* is an 1853 memoir and slave narrative by Solomon Northup as told to and written by David Wilson.
- Watch a movie like *Remember the Titans* or *The Best of Enemies* to see how people can change and combat their "isms."
- The next time you see someone act racist, sexist, tribalist, or materialist toward someone else, stick up for the person being attacked.
- Did anything come to mind that you felt you should do as you read this section? Did you underline or make a note of something you should do? If so, make a reminder for yourself to do it!

Random Notes, Doodles, and Reflections

CHAPTER 12

Getting Distracted by Virtual Gimmicks

"Social media is like crack—immediately gratifying and hugely addictive."

—Gary Vaynerchuk

The most important freedom you can have is the freedom to choose how you spend your time. Think about prison: One of the reasons it is so demoralizing is that you have little say over what you do all day, every day. It's the same with people who suffer from drug addiction. In prison, someone else is making decisions about your time for you, and as a drug user, your addiction is choosing how you spend your time.

It's also the same with social media.

"Okay, but are you saying social media is like going to prison or using drugs?"

In terms of greatly influencing how you spend your time and

attention? Absolutely. Think about how much money you pay to use TikTok or Instagram. Nothing. How do these huge companies make mega money off the time you spend on their platforms? They sell your time and attention to people who want you to see what they are selling. Take Meta, Instagram's parent company, for example. Advertising revenue, which accounts for the lion's share of Meta's total revenue, was more than $25 billion in 2020 (back then the company was known as Facebook).[1] For comparison, in 2020, McDonald's worldwide revenue was roughly $19 billion. To continue making these ginormous amounts of money, Meta and other social media companies are heavily invested in getting (and keeping) your attention. Think about all the dings, beeps, and vibrations you get on your phone that try to draw your attention back to it.

Also, think about how, as soon as you're watching one video, TikTok and YouTube immediately show you something else you can watch. They want you hooked. They want you to stick around and keep watching for as long as possible. They want you to indicate that you "like" the things that you see, so they can understand how to send you more things that can keep your attention.

Here are some questions that will help gauge how impactful social media is in your daily life:

What is the first thing you do when you wake up?

____

____

____

How much time do you spend on social media each day?

____

____

____

When you are reading, praying, studying, or even talking with a friend, do you stop to check your phone as soon as it pings?

____

____

____

I heard someone compare the internet to a mall (you guys remember what those things are, right?). I thought this was a good comparison—up to a point. What is the purpose of a mall? To get you to come and spend money. There are very few things to do at the mall that don't involve spending money (you can see the old people walking in the mall, and sometimes there might be some weird government thing there so you can renew your car tabs), but even if you just go with your friends to hang out, you are still tempted to buy all kinds of stuff. Kind of like social media with your attention, right?

The thing about the mall when I was your age was that I had to ask my parents if I could go. Then, I had to find my way there (I remember taking the bus a few times to the mall). Finally, I had to have money to buy stuff.

Compare that to social media today: We don't need money to spend. We don't have to get on the bus. We have our phones with us almost all the time. It's constantly on and constantly seeking our attention. That is its goal: our attention and our time.

Do you know what a carnival barker is? If you go to a fair or carnival, these are the folks working the games, running the stalls that sell you food and trinkets. They are all trying to get your attention, so you come over and see what they are selling and get you to buy or participate. Some of these folks can be intense. The internet is much more intense than the mall and even the carnival barker. There are thousands of folks barking at you for your attention—every day, every minute that you are on your phone. What a huge challenge.

How likely is empathetic listening to occur via social media? Most unlikely. Writer David Brooks trashed social media as a place for effective communication: "We don't communicate from our hearts and souls on the internet; we communicate through our egos, through comparison. My life is better than yours—that's Instagram. Your opinions are stupider than mine—that's Twitter [now X as you know]. We are not programmed, and we weren't created to communicate on this shallow level."[2]

In the 1500s, Swiss physician Paracelsus discovered a principle of toxicology (the study of poisons) that we still use today:

The dose makes the poison.

In other words, all chemicals—even water—can be toxic if too much is eaten, drunk, or absorbed. You can tell from this book that I spend some time on social media and *am* on social media myself. I use the internet quite a bit. I am not saying we shouldn't use social media or the internet, but we need to carefully choose how and how often we use it—our dose.

So, what does the intentional, appropriate use of the internet and social media look like? Well, it depends. A recent study followed a sample of teenage girls (about thirteen years old) who used social media for at least two to three hours per day at the beginning of the study. As they increased their social media use, researchers found these girls were at a higher clinical risk for suicide as emerging adults.[3] Another study found that what teens see on social media affects their mental health more than the time they spend online. On days when a teen experienced more negative things—like hurtful comments or online drama—they were more likely to have suicidal thoughts. But on days when they had more positive interactions, like receiving supportive messages or fun posts, they were less likely to think about suicide.[4]

Reject social media's short-term pleasures that rob you of your attention, foster unnecessary and harmful comparisons, and keep you addicted to its short-lived dopamine hits (dings, likes, and flashes). Instead, think about how you can use social media and the internet to aid your leadership over the long term, for example: building relationships, spreading positive messages, and creating community.

Social media's Kryptonite is you exercising your freedom to choose how you positively spend your time. Consistently. Remember the power of compounding? Good internet habits will reward you; bad internet habits will suck you into a meaningless, self-absorbed world that uses you and your attention for its own gain. And don't worry, we all get sucked into the internet rabbit hole sometimes. Don't beat yourself up about it. Mistakes are part of the journey, as we discuss in the next chapter. What you do next is way more important than any misstep.

Key Points:

- ✓ The internet and social media are filled with people and companies vying for your attention, and they are very good at drawing you in and keeping you there.
- ✓ We need to make wise choices about how and how often we will use social media and the internet. The dose makes the poison.
- ✓ Good internet habits will reward you; bad internet habits will suck you into a meaningless, self-absorbed world that uses you and your attention for its own gain.
- ✓ The more time we spend in the real world on relationships and leadership, the more effective and rewarding both will be.

Ponder

- How is the internet and social media helping or hurting you in nurturing healthy relationships?
- What good habits have you picked up on social media? What bad habits have you picked up on social media?
- If you had to get rid of one social media app, which one would it be? Why?

Do

- Talk to your friends about how social media is making your life better and worse. Together, identify one habit you can all develop to make your social media time better for you.
- Make a list of the things you are doing on social media that help you become a better leader and a worse leader.
- Create a plan about how you will use social media for good and implement it. Try it for one day, then discuss your plan with a parent or trusted adult to get their input.
- Did anything come to mind that you felt you should do as you read this section? Did you underline or make a note of something you should do? If so, make a reminder for yourself to do it!

Random Notes, Doodles, and Reflections

CHAPTER 13

Mistakes Are Part of the Journey

"Mistakes are the stairs we climb to reach success."

—Tim Fargo

Are you thoroughly overwhelmed? Please don't be. *Choose* not to be. As I've mentioned before, this is not a book that you read once and it changes your life. Reading this book is merely one step on your path to greatness.

Just keep plugging away.

We saved one of the great leadership superpowers for last: learning from our experiences, including mistakes. Another name for that? Growth.

First, let's get some perspective with a heat check. Have you ever read a book or watched something and been so inspired that you thought you were that hero and could do in real life what they did in the movie? I have—way too many times.

I see a clip about Michael Jordan and think, "Yeah, I can do that," and go out and try and shoot like him, or try to make some MJ Nerf hoop dunks, or just dream about doing it in my mind. Then reality kicks in. Heat check! Seeing a clip about MJ doesn't magically turn me into him. Just like reading a book about Beyoncé isn't going to make me able to sing like her, or googling inspiring stories about George Washington isn't going to magically make me president of the United States, or stop telling lies. However, all these things can put me on the road to becoming something different from what I am. How? By being inspired, being a learner, being a worker, and growing from the mistakes I make along the way.

Second, none of us are born leaders (so many folks have said this, I am not even sure who to attribute the words to). Jim Dolan, a psychotherapist with over forty years of experience as a leadership coach for lawyers and executives (so basically, he teaches old people), said, "Leadership must be grown into. There is no other way."[1] If old people need to learn leadership, then we know young folks like you do, too. This also means that we all can become leaders.

We become leaders by having principles and choosing to live by them (i.e., having integrity), choosing to feed the White Wolf, being on Team Sun, being empathetic listeners, working on good habits, and reaping the rewards that grow from those habits.

We also learn how to lead by doing the wrong thing.

Mistakes are an important part of the process of becoming a leader. Let's go back to empathy for a minute. If you had never made a mistake, how could you relate to me when I share one of my mistakes? How could you understand the embarrassment, the pain, the desire to go back in time and erase that experience and do the right thing this time around? You couldn't.

How did you learn not to touch something hot? Was it your mom or dad, or someone else, telling you? "Don't touch, HOT!" Or was it by touching the stove and burning your hand? Which experience taught you more? Maybe that is not a fair question. Perhaps a better question is, Did you learn differently from those two experiences?

When we make a mistake, we have choices: pretend it didn't happen, fight over whether it happened, ignore it, blame others, run, double down on the mistake so it becomes a habit (yikes), or learn from our mistake. Great leaders ultimately choose this last option. Making that choice requires us to accept that we are human, be willing to examine our lives to see our mistakes, and acknowledge the pain that comes with them. Being willing to recognize our mistakes is a fail-safe pattern for growth.

When we make a mistake, the growth process can look like this:

1. Recognize that you've made a mistake.
2. Make amends (it could be as simple as saying you are sorry or replacing something you broke or stole).
3. Learn from it.
4. Do better next time.
5. Repeat as often as necessary (it will be quite often for most of us).

Let's look at a simple example: I lost my temper and punched my brother.

1. **Recognize the mistake.** I should not punch my brother. He made me mad by going into my bedroom (where there is a sign that says he is NOT ALLOWED) and touching my stuff. Yet, that doesn't make it right to punch him. He is my little

brother—I could have badly hurt him, or made him think punching people was okay. That was my mistake. I should not do that again.

2. **Make amends.** I told my little brother that I was sorry for hitting him, that what I did was not right, and that I should not have done it.
3. **Learn.** This step can be challenging. For anyone who plays a sport and watches films of prior games to see what you did right or wrong and what needs improvement, this is a good analogy. Rewind the incident in your head, including the things leading up to the mistake and the things after it. You can probably identify some things that you did or did not do that made it more likely that you were going to make a bad choice.

   For example, I could see that I stayed out too late the night before, so I was still tired Saturday morning when my little brother went into my room. I was hungry, too, since I had not had breakfast. I was a little bored as well. I didn't have a good handle on what I was going to do that day. Those circumstances put me in a position where maybe I was a bit on edge and looking for something to do, like get mad at my little brother.

   One option would be to try and address some causes leading up to the mistake. When I ran the film in my head, I saw the reasons that led to the punch—things I could change so I was less likely to hit my brother the next time he came into my room uninvited. The great thing about being a learner is that there are so many things to learn. If you have the desire to learn from your mistakes, you absolutely will.

4. **Do better.** I admitted I made a mistake. I apologized to my brother, and I examined what I could learn from the situation. I realized that I needed to do better next time. When I caught my little brother going into my bedroom again, guess what? I just yelled at him. I didn't punch him. PROGRESS. IMPROVEMENT. CHANGE. IT WORKED!
5. **Repeat as necessary.** Some might say, "Well, you still yelled at him, which is not nice." That is true. That means I should continue working through this process and continue to get better. But I *did* do better. IT WORKED! I learned and grew from my mistakes. But even if I had punched my brother again, that wouldn't have stopped me from working to improve. The only way to fail at this is to stop trying!

What I've learned as a dad, a husband, a lawyer, a coach, and a human being is that perfection cannot always be our standard. If we set the goal of perfection in all that we do, we are going to be crushed under the weight of our mistakes. Perfection in everything is simply not possible for us humans.

Think about your most admired role model, coach, or teacher to whom you dedicated this book. I don't think that person expects perfection from you in all that you do. They may expect one rep to be perfect. They may expect one song to be played perfectly. They also know that achieving that perfection in one thing, at one time, results from many imperfect reps. Sometimes the goal of perfection can destroy our desire to even begin down the road of trying to do something better. Perfection is NOT the goal. Improving and working to be better is. Don't let your imperfection frustrate your growth. Think about it: Perfection does not allow for growth.

The beauty of learning from your mistakes is that you are making *different* mistakes. That means you are constantly growing, learning, and improving. The lessons you learn are likely more refined because the changes you have made from your past mistakes have compounded so that you *are* progressing. Remember, good habits have the compounding effect of miraculous growth.

Great leaders live lives of constant improvement. A great habit that leads to growth and improvement is recognizing and learning from our mistakes.

Key Points:

- ✓ None of us are perfect.
- ✓ None of us are born leaders.
- ✓ If you have the desire to learn from your mistakes, you absolutely will.
- ✓ Great leaders live lives of constant improvement

Ponder 🤔

- What would life be like if you were perfect? What would the world be like if everyone were perfect?
- Other than your most recent ones (perhaps they're still too raw), what are some of your worst mistakes? What have you learned from these mistakes?
- How do you feel when someone hurts you, then apologizes and asks for your forgiveness? What might prevent you from apologizing to someone for a mistake you made that hurt them?

Do

- Apologize to someone whom you know you need to apologize to.
- Next time you make a mistake, don't be so hard on yourself. Acknowledging our mistakes is a sign of growth!
- Talk to someone whom you believe does not make mistakes. Write down your experience talking to this person.
- Did anything come to mind that you felt you should do as you read this section? Did you underline or make a note of something you should do? If so, make a reminder for yourself to do it!

Random Notes, Doodles, and Reflections

CONCLUSION

Keep On Leading!

"The most powerful story in the world is the one you tell yourself."
—Shane Parrish

Experience is a great teacher if you are humble. When you understand you don't have all the answers, that you have much to learn, and there are many who can teach you. *That's when* you start developing as a person and a leader.

Everything I have learned in my life comes from others. So many people have shared ideas, principles, practices, and examples with me that have helped me grow as a husband, father, son, brother, player, coach, attorney, and human being. That's why I could not have written this book twenty or even ten years ago.

Now, I am passing these things on to you. Will you do the same? Take whatever portion of your leadership progress that is good or helpful to you and do something to pass it along. What does that look like? Whatever you want it to look like. For me, it's been writing this book. The ways and things we relay to others are as different as each of us are as people.

Here is the simple leadership plan I am passing on to you: Do.

Choose a "Do" from the end of chapter 5 on integrity and then *do it*. Here they are:

- Identify someone you know who has integrity. Compliment them. Ask them how they work to develop integrity.
- Think about someone you look up to. What principles do you think they try to live by? Take one of those principles and apply it to your life tomorrow.
- Think about an issue that you have been grappling with. Is there a principle that you can apply to it, or the circumstances surrounding the issue that will help you work through it? If you think there is, try it! Here is a recent real-life story. Adrian Rodriguez, a California teenager, found a woman's purse in a grocery store parking lot. Adrian could have lived by the belief that "finders keepers" justified a decision to keep the purse and money in it. Instead, Adrian acted on his principle of empathy for others. He considered the woman's potential distress from losing her purse and decided to return it to its owner.

Don't overthink it. Don't be paralyzed by not knowing where to start. Choose to lead. Be a leader. Then, do it again tomorrow, and two times the next day. Make a mistake—and then learn from that mistake. Remember, mistakes are inevitable. Learning from them is how we grow as leaders and flourish. As you keep doing things that leaders do, you will become an effective leader.

Know that you are already a leader. You are just becoming more of one. A better one. You are being a leader more minutes out of the day, seeing things you didn't see before. You're feeding your White Wolf. You're choosing Team Sun.

Keep on leading. It was a snowflake. Now, it's a snowball. Next, it's an avalanche. It is working! You are a leader. I see it. Others see it. I feel it. Others feel it. You are helping them. You are listening to them. You are serving them.

Mother Teresa, known for her dedication to serving others, is often quoted as saying, "A life not lived for others is not a life." Serving others is essential to living a great life and to being a great leader. Mother Teresa was a great leader. You are a great leader. Your choices can change the world for good.

Sometimes we are the rat in the jar who needs to keep swimming (or in this case, keep leading). Sometimes we are the hand that picks the rat up—that touches someone, recognizes them, lifts them out of the water, and shows them that the situation is not impending doom. As leaders, our acts of service—small and large—can be the source of life-changing hope.

I used to think so-and-so was a jerk, but I have been listening to him, trying to understand him, hearing a little more about where he is coming from, and serving him. I have come to see he is fighting a hard fight. He has problems; some of them feel like mine, and some of them are quite different. He isn't rude to me anymore. Our relationship has changed as I chose to be a leader, the kind of leader who saw beyond tribalism and beyond me, me, me. I am the kind of leader who began to view myself and others as people with potential, deserving of encouragement and being heard.

Living this type of leadership is fulfilling. My rewards have been more peace, more satisfaction, and more happiness from a place inside me that longs to be happy, and quite different from the fleeting emotions that come from likes, a new car, fresh kicks, or any other material thing I buy. It comes from my actions matching my heart.

Being a leader has shifted my perspective from "just me" to focusing on my family, my friends, and even folks who I thought were my enemies. Now I see their potential, which has also given me a new perspective on *my* potential. It is something that I want to share with them, not keep hidden, not run away from, but embrace and spread everywhere. I can go anywhere on this earth and feel like I can spread some sunshine.

So just start. Do the easy stuff. Do the hard stuff. Make mistakes. Don't beat yourself up. Lift others when you are down. Also, let others lift you when you are down.

Did you come up with your slogan/catchphrase/mantra/hype song yet? If so, put it here 👇

If not, can you give it some thought and write something later? Even if it is not perfect, it's a start. You can come back and change it, update it, or create multiple ones. Keep tracking the words that motivate you as you move along your leadership path. It is a wonderful journey with highs, lows, and lots of things in between.

I asked my kids about my slogans, and apparently, I have lots of them. My favorite and most enduring is probably "Fish On!" I used to fish quite a bit. I grew up with a river close enough that I could ride my bike. Sometimes, I would skip school and go fishing with my dad. When we hooked a fish, we were supposed to say, "Fish On!" At that point, everyone got excited and echoed it back. It was a blast. Back in the day, with my fishing buddies, we would say, "Fish On!" just to get each other excited or cracking up. When I need a lift or some energy, "Fish On!" will do it for me.

Last thing before I go: Earlier, I talked about "your unlimited potential." This is not hype. We are all finite. We are all going to die. So, what do I mean by "your unlimited potential"? The ripples of your leadership, your influence, can continue well beyond your lifetime. Your encouraging influence can endure long after you are gone. What a blessing, not just that you can do this, but that you can take great hope in knowing that your service will last beyond your mortality.

And now . . . tag, you're it.

Keep leading!

Your service to others will send impactful ripples that will compound for good.

Fish On!

Hooray, you made it!

Now, please take two more minutes to scan the QR code and complete a quick follow-up survey.

Your insights help us understand how this book is shaping leaders like you. Thanks again for being part of the journey.

Epilogue

Books change lives. Why do I say this? Because it happened to me. I shared an issue that I was struggling with in my church's men's group once. The group's response was somewhat meh. But my friend, Ron Trogdon, thoughtfully called me later. I talked, and he listened. He suggested a book for me. It was *Spiritual Roots of Human Relations* by Stephen Covey, and it made a huge impact (that's why I've quoted it so much in this book).

I read it. I wrote in it. I reread the sections. I highlighted in it. I thought about it. The book was near my bedside many nights. The book helped me, as Ron believed it would. In a simple and meaningful way, Ron led me.

I don't even remember the issue that led Ron to give me the book. But I remember Ron. And I remember the book. Problems may come and go, but caring leaders and their inspiring books stay with you forever.

So, be like Ron. Care. Listen. Reach out. Share. Lead. Read books. And when you read an inspiring one, share it. Hint. Hint.

Acknowledgments

Bringing this book to life was a team effort. I am deeply grateful for the contributions of many remarkable individuals who have shaped my understanding of leadership and inspired me to share it with others.

At the very heart of my gratitude is my wife, Bonnie. Her unwavering kindness, unselfishness, and work ethic are a great inspiration and source of strength to me. When my self-doubt arose, Bonnie was a reliable cheerleader.

I would like to extend special thanks to two groups whose influence is woven throughout this book:

My mentors: teachers from elementary school through college, Scout leaders, coaches, my friends, law professors, colleagues from Kirkland & Ellis and Summit Law Group, church teachers and leaders, and dedicated peers from various nonprofits I've had the privilege to collaborate with. My family has also profoundly shaped my leadership journey. If you fall into one of these categories, you have provided me with invaluable guidance and support.

You, inspiring young leaders: the exceptional youth in our community, athletes I've had so much fun coaching, the youth in our church congregations, my kids, siblings, and cousins, and my fellow lacrosse coaches. Your passion, drive, and potential fuel my optimism and hope for our future.

Another shout-out to those who generously devoted time to reviewing early drafts and offering valuable insights: Bonnie, Caitlin, McKay, Carter, Chloe, Quinn, Ty Draney, Kate Blatter, and my mom. Your thoughtful feedback helped shape this book. And Will's off-the-cuff remarks drove me to make it better.

To the dedicated professionals who transformed my early manuscript into the finished guide you are holding now: Marni Senak, Danielle Goodman, CW Patrick, Bobby Hoyt, and the remarkable team at Amplify. Your expertise took this book to the next level, and I am thrilled to see its impact.

Thank you all for enriching my life and contributing to this work. This book is a celebration of your influence and leadership.

Notes

Preface

1 A link to the study on rats is provided here:

2 Curt P. Richter, "On the Phenomenon of Sudden Death in Animals and Man," *Psychosomatic Medicine* 19, no. 3 (May 1957).

3 Storyteller Bruce Herschensohn describes it like this: "We have now got the next generation into debt—four trillion dollars [in late 2024, the number has ballooned to $36 trillion]. I don't see a conscience in this country, and I think we all ought to have a very heavy conscience . . . Those kids are going to be born. We're all going to be gone. And they're going to say, 'My god, what did they do to us? . . . That's worse than being a common thief. A common thief, you can hope gets

prosecuted; you can hope you get some of the material back. They're not going to get any of it back."

Timothy Sandefur, "Bruce Herschensohn, RIP," The Dispatch, December 2, 2020, https://thedispatch.com/p/bruce-herschensohn-rip.

Chapter 1

1 This devil-on-shoulder image comes from watching Donald Duck cartoons, where Donald Duck had an angel (white with a halo) and a devil (red with horns) competing for Donald Duck's attention. This QR code will take you to one of those cartoons:

Chapter 4

1 Apparently, the Natural Helpers program died due to a lack of funding but may be making a comeback. More information here:

2 Information on the Hope Squad can be found here:

3 David Boynton and Marija Vasileva-Blazev, "Half of the World's Population Is Under 30—but They Have Little Say over the Decisions That Shape Their Future. It's Time for Young People to Be Seen and Heard in the Halls of Power," *Fortune*, January 25, 2023, https://fortune.com/europe/2023/01/25/

world-population-little-say-decisions-future-young-people-seen-and-heard-halls-of-power-boynton-vasileva-blazev/.

4 "10 Things You Didn't Know About the World's Population," The United Nations, April 10, 2015, https://www.un.org/youthaffairs/en.

5 Dustin Albert et al., "The Teenage Brain: Peer Influences on Adolescent Decision Making," *Sage Journals* 22, no. 2 (2013).

6 Laurence Steinberg, "How Peers Affect the Teenage Brain," *Psychology Today*, February 3, 2011, https://www.psychologytoday.com/us/blog/you-and-your-adolescent/201102/how-peers-affect-the-teenage-brain.

7 Peter L. Benson, "Fragile Foundation: The State of Developmental Assets Among American Youth," Minneapolis: Search Institute, 2011, 7 and Table 2.1, 136 and Table A.2.

8 Petr Badura et al., "A Focus on Adolescent Social Contexts in Europe, Central Asia and Canada Health Behaviour in School-Aged Children International Report from the 2021/2022 Survey," Copenhagen: WHO Regional Office for Europe, 2024, 4–12.

9 Writer James Chapman created a list of the most-read books in the world based on the number of copies each book sold over the last fifty years. He found that the Bible far outsold any other book, with a whopping 3.9 billion copies sold. Second place is Chairman Mao, at 820 million copies. Jennifer Polland, "The 10 Most Read Books in the World [Infographic]," *Business Insider*, December 27, 2012, https://www.businessinsider.com/the-top-10-most-read-booksin-the-world-infographic-2012-12?type=social.

10 Josephus, "Antiquities of the Jews. Sacred Texts," book 5, chapter 10, section 4, n.d.

11 Áine Cain, "17 People Who Accomplished Incredible Things at a Shockingly Young Age," *Business Insider*, January 9, 2017, https://www.businessinsider.com/

people-who-accomplished-incredible-things-young-2017-1#nellie-bly-exposed-a-dysfunctional-mental-asylum-at-23-14.

12 Sam Boggon, "Trudy Ederle: American Swimmer Who Became the First Woman to Swim the English Channel," Sky Sports, July 20, 2024, https://www.skysports.com/olympics/news/15234/13176579/trudy-ederle-american-swimmer-who-became-the-first-woman-to-swim-the-english-channel#:~:text=New%20York%20City%20honoured%20her,out%20to%20cheer%20her%20success.

13 "8 Young People Who Changed History and the World," Shutterstock, January 24, 2020, https://www.shutterstock.com/blog/young-people-who-changed-history.

Chapter 5

1 Mark Twain, *Adventures of Huckleberry Finn*, chapter 31 (Charles L. Webster and Company, 1885), 204.

2 Adam Teicher, "Success, Trust and Burnt Ends: Why Everyone Loves Kansas City Chiefs Coach Andy Reid," *ESPN*, January 21, 2021, https://www.espn.com/nfl/story/_/id/30424487/why-everyone-loves-chiefs-coach-andy-reid.

3 The analogy is not perfect regarding the stars, since Earth's axis changes over many years. "As a result, 5,000 years ago . . . the North Star was Thuban. Similarly, in 12,000 years, the star Vega (in the constellation Lyra) will be the North Star."

Rich Schuler, "What Exactly Is the North Star?" *Scientific American*, January 3, 2006, https://www.scientificamerican.com/article/what-exactly-is-the-north/#:~:text=The%20North%20Star%2C%20or%20Polaris,Polaris%20occupies%20a%20special%20place.

4 Lewis Carroll and John Tenniel, in *Alice's Adventures in Wonderland* (The Macmillan Company, 1904), 51.

5 "Good Deed: SoCal Teen Praised for Tracking Down Owner of Purse That Was Left at Local Ralphs," *ABC*, June 29, 2022.

Chapter 6

1 Twain, *Adventures of Huckleberry Finn.*

2 Wikimedia Foundation, "Two Wolves," Wikipedia, accessed March 26, 2025, https://en.wikipedia.org/wiki/Two_Wolves.

Chapter 7

1 Tim O'Connor, "The Foundation of Leadership with Drew Dudley," Results, May 9, 2022, https://blog.unleashresults.com/the-foundation-of-leadership-with-drew-dudley.

2 In pop culture, this quotation is attributed to Albert Einstein. ChatGPT-4o says there is no credible evidence to support Einstein saying this.

3 M. B. Roberts, "How Many Snowflakes Does It Take to Build a Snowman?" Parade, December 14, 2018, https://parade.com/723450/m-b-roberts/how-many-snowflakes-does-it-take-to-build-a-snowman/.

4 Edward Alfred Steiner, *Tolstoy: The Man* (Wentworth Press, 2016).

5 Stephen R. Covey, *Spiritual Roots of Human Relations* (Desert Books Co., 1971).

Chapter 8

1 Steven Handel, "Why No One Is Normal and How to Focus on Individual Uniqueness," *The Motion Machine*, n.d., https://www.theemotionmachine.com/why-no-one-is-normal-and-how-to-focus-on-individual-uniqueness/.

2 Handel, "Individual Uniqueness."

3 Judith Rich Harris, *No Two Alike: Human Nature and Human Individuality* (W. W. Norton & Company, 2007), 261–262.

4 Elizabeth Dinan, "Drunken Portsmouth Hobo, Now a Sober Author," Seacoastonline, July 3, 2016, https://www.seacoastonline.com/news/20160703/drunken-portsmouth-hobo-now-sober-author.

5 "The research shows that diversity allows groups to think better about critical problems. It is the friction of coming from different backgrounds and looking at issues from different vantage points that creates a productive energy."

John Blake, "A Drained Swimming Pool Shows How Racism Harms White People, Too," *CNN*, March 6, 2021, https://www.cnn.com/2021/03/05/us/heather-mcghee-racism-white-people-blake/index.html.

6 *The Udana*, edited by Princeton.edu, translated by Randy Wang, March 19, 1995, https://web.archive.org/web/20060825152508/http://www.cs.princeton.edu/~rywang/berkeley/258/parable.html.

7 Morgan Housel, "Ideas That Changed My Life," Collaborative Fund, December 7, 2022, https://www.collaborativefund.com/blog/ideas-that-changed-my-life/.

Chapter 9

1 "New Report Suggests That over 1 in 3 Americans Face 'Serious Loneliness' During the Pandemic, Including over 60% of Young Adults," Harvard University, Making Caring Common Project., February 9, 2021, https://static1.squarespace.com/static/5b7c56e-255b02c683659fe43/t/6021781b5ef8c15ffa215ee3/1612806171358/Loneliness+in+America+press+release+2021_02_08.pdf.

2 Travis Hanson, *The Next Few Years Will Change Your Life* (Desert Book, 2012), 108–110.

3 Covey, *Spiritual Roots of Human Relations*, 131.

4 Ignacy Krasicki, “The Master and His Dog,” in *Fables and Parables* (1779).

5 Johann Hari, “Everything You Think You Know About Addiction Is Wrong,” TED Talk, January 15, 2021, YouTube, 00:00 -14:32, https://www.ted.com/talks/johann_hari_everything_you_think_you_know_about_addiction_is_wrong?referrer=playlist-new_thoughts_on_addiction#t-869000.

6 Covey, *Spiritual Roots of Human Relations*, 117.

Chapter 10

1 Here is a link to that video:

2 *Id.*

3 Simon Sinek, *Leaders Eat Last: Why Some Teams Pull Together and Others Don't* (Portfolio, 2017). Contains quote from Lieutenant General George Flynn, USMC, “The cost of leadership is self-interest.”

4 “Are You Among the Best Humans?” Human Initiative, February 15, 2022, https://human-initiative.org/are-you-among-the-best-humans/?lang=en.

5 Covey, *Spiritual Roots of Human Relations*, 201.

Chapter 11

1 “ism (n.),” *Merriam-Webster, s.v.*, accessed April 11, 2025, https://www.merriam-webster.com/dictionary/ism.

2 Here's a link to the podcast:

Todd Simkin, interview by Shane Parrish, *The Knowledge Project*, episode 119, "Making Better Decisions," September 7, 2021, https://www.youtube.com/watch?v=XGk-qXHK8ZE&t=2s.

3 If you want to better understand the origins of the Black People Love Watermelon trope, this article is helpful:

William R. Black, "How Watermelons Became a Racist Trope," *Atlantic*, December 8, 2014, https://www.theatlantic.com/national/archive/2014/12/how-watermelons-became-a-racist-trope/383529/.

4 John Blake, "A Drained Swimming Pool Shows How Racism Harms White People, Too," *CNN*, March 6, 2021, https://www.cnn.com/2021/03/05/us/heather-mcghee-racism-white-people-blake/index.html.

5 Adam Grant (@AdamMGrant), "Sexual harassment isn't driven by a desire for women. It's motivated by a desire for power over women. Data: assertive women face more sexual harassment—especially in male-dominated workplaces. The problem is not self-control. It's a culture that normalizes control over women," X, October 7, 2021, 8:13 am, https://x.com/AdamMGrant/status/1446086301309149190.

6 George Monbiot, "Materialism: A System That Eats Us from the Inside Out," *Guardian*, December 9, 2013, https://www.theguardian.com/commentisfree/2013/dec/09/materialism-system-eats-us-from-inside-out.

7 Rik Pieters, "Bidirectional Dynamics of Materialism and Loneliness: Not Just a Vicious Cycle," *Journal of Consumer Research* 40, no. 4 (2013): 31–615, doi:10.1086/671564.

8 Monbiot, "Materialism."

Chapter 12

1 Sarah E. Needleman, "Facebook's Ad Business Drives Surge in Revenue, Following Google's Act," *Wall Street Journal*, April 28, 2021, https://www.wsj.com/articles/facebook-fb-1q-earnings-report-2021-11619610405#:~:-text=Advertising%20revenue%2C%20which%20accounts%20for,billion%2C%20or%20%243.30%20a%20share.

2 David Brooks, "Finding the Road to Character," BYU, Provo, Utah, October 22, 2019, https://www.youtube.com/watch?v=cisBl3yXJFs.

3 Christie Allen, "10-Year BYU Study Shows Elevated Suicide Risk from Excess Social Media Time for Young Teen Girls," news.byu.edu, February 3, 2021, https://news.byu.edu/intellect/10-year-byu-studyshows-elevated-suicide-risk-from-excess-social-media-time-foryoung-teen-girls.

4 Jessica Leigh Hamilton et al., "Positive and Negative Social Media Experiences and Proximal Risk for Suicidal Ideation in Adolescents," *Journal of Child Psychology and Psychiatry and Allied Disciplines* 65, no. 12 (2024): 1580–1589, https://colab.ws/articles/10.1111%2Fjcpp.13996#:~:-text=Significant%20within%E2%80%90person%20effects%20of%20negative,SI%20on%20next%E2%80%90day%20SM%20experiences.

Chapter 13

1 Jim Dolan, "The Hard Truth About Authentic Leadership: Insights from an Executive Psychotherapist, Corporate Counsel," Law.com, August 16, 2021, https://www.law.com/corpcounsel/2021/08/16/the-hard-truth-about-authentic-leadership-insights-from-an-executive-psychotherapist/?slreturn=20250411180422.

About the Author

Chad Mitchell has spent the past thirty years working alongside youth—as a coach, teacher, mentor, and father—witnessing the incredible impact of young people leading one another. His passion is simple and powerful: to help youth step into leadership not someday, but now!

From the sports field and classrooms to summer camps and youth groups, Chad has seen what happens when young people are empowered to take the lead. His message is clear: Youth are not just the leaders of tomorrow; they are leaders now.

His book, *Change Your Game: Empowering Young Leaders to Ditch Doubt, Find Their Voice, and Impact the World*, is a dynamic and practical guide designed to inspire youth to discover their potential and grow into confident, authentic, and effective leaders. It's built on the belief that leadership is not about age—it's about self-awareness, confidence, and action.

Chad has presented these ideas to high school students, youth leadership camps, sports teams, and small groups, always with the same goal: to help youth realize they have the power to make an impact right where they are.

He and his wife Bonnie live in Richland, Washington. They've raised six kids and are proud grandparents to four granddaughters (so far). Chad's mission is to spark a global movement of youth leaders—creating ripples of goodness that roll worldwide.